Assessing Student Learning in the Disciplines

Edited by Trudy W. Banta

Assessment
UPdate
COLLECTIONS

Published by Jossey-Bass
A Wiley Imprint
989 Market Street, San Francisco, CA 94103-1741   www.josseybass.com

Jossey-Bass books and products are available through most bookstores. To contact Jossey-Bass
directly call our Customer Care Department within the U.S. at 800-956-7739, outside the
U.S. at 317-572-3986, or fax 317-572-4002.

Jossey-Bass also publishes its books in a variety of electronic formats. Some content that
appears in print may not be available in electronic books.

Library of Congress Cataloging-in-Publication Data available upon request

Printed in the United States of America
FIRST EDITION
PB Printing   10 9 8 7 6 5 4 3 2 1

Contents

Assessment in Disciplines Not Subject to Accreditation

Standardized Measures of Student Learning in the Major

Introduction: Assessing Student Learning in the Disciplines

Trudy W. Banta

As Barbara Wright wisely observes in the first article in this collection, "The way to a faculty member's head is through the discipline. . . . The discipline is where a faculty member lives. . . . It is love for and expertise in the discipline that (faculty) hope to cultivate in their students."

Faculty Development for Assessment

Because faculty members' thinking is immersed in the discipline(s) they teach, it often makes good sense to begin an assessment initiative at a college or university by focusing on student learning in the discipline, or academic major. In her article, Wright describes an approach to providing a key ingredient for any assessment initiative—faculty development. At an annual meeting of the New England Educational Assessment Network, faculty in three social sciences—psychology, sociology, and political science—were given opportunities to discuss the development of learning outcomes for students, the selection or design of assessment methods appropriate to the disciplines, the use of assessment findings to improve teaching and learning, and possibilities for turning work in assessment into scholarly presentations and publications in disciplinary journals.

Regional accreditation requirements and state mandates for accountability provide powerful catalysts for faculty involvement in outcomes assessment. The professional development network of Wright's colleagues in New England was established in part to serve as a source of support for faculty seeking to accommodate a new emphasis by the regional accreditor, the New England Association of Schools and Colleges, on evidence of institutional accountability for student learning outcomes. In the second article I write about the responses of faculty at the University of Tennessee, Knoxville (UTK), to the performance funding mandate of the state legislature and the Tennessee Higher Education Commission. While some faculty responded negatively to that early external mandate, others saw it as an opportunity to improve curricula, instruction, and ultimately student learning. With the assistance of faculty development provided by the Learning Research Center at UTK and a small competitive grant program provided by the provost, faculty in over 100 major fields selected or designed assessment strategies for seniors over a period of five years. In some cases, external experts in the discipline were brought to Knoxville to work with faculty on such assessment methods as case studies, in-basket exercises, field-experience evaluations, and senior design projects. Improvements in academic programs and teaching methods at UTK that can be attributed to the application of assessment findings are well documented in this article and in other publications on performance funding in Tennessee.

Student Competence as a Basis for Assessment

An essential step in developing an assessment process that leads to improvement is to state desired learning outcomes for students. Some faculty consider the identification of learning outcomes so important that they speak in terms of the dimensions of competence that characterize their graduates and refer to their curricula as competence-based. My article on student competence summarizes the experiences of three institutions in basing their curricula and approaches to assessment on statements of competence. One of the institutions bases assessment on six liberal-arts learning outcomes. The others involve employers in defining, assessing, and improving student competence in a variety of majors.

Since *Assessment Update* was first published in 1989, there has been pervasive interest in describing, teaching, and assessing competence, and then using assessment findings to further enhance learning. In an early issue in 1990 we reported on the use of a matrix by agricultural business faculty "to assess congruence between course content and competence areas identified for undergraduate majors. Course titles are listed across the top of the matrix and 17 competence areas are listed on the left side." This was the first of a number of articles over the years that have recommended the use of matrices to ensure that important learning outcomes are taught and assessed in multiple contexts across the curriculum in a given major.

Sixteen years later, *Assessment Update* authors are still focused on student competence. In 2006 David Shupe told readers how faculty can identify the learning outcomes associated with competence, develop rubrics that describe competence, and then use these rubrics to evaluate the work students do in their courses. The use of common rubrics permits cross-curricular electronic aggregation of competence data that can help students track their own progress and help faculty detect course and curricular strengths and weaknesses.

Assessment in Disciplines Subject to Accreditation

In fields like nursing, education, social work, and some subfields in engineering and business, the competence of graduates must be assured through licensure or certification because the influence of practitioners on public health and welfare is substantial. The need to provide quality assurance among graduates and practitioners, among other factors, has led to the formation of professional associations in these fields. A major responsibility of these associations is to accredit collegiate educational programs, and assessing student attainment of specified outcomes has long been a focus in the accreditation process. Thus it is not surprising that on most campuses faculty in disciplines subject to accreditation are the pioneers and trend-setters in developing approaches to outcomes assessment.

Just such a pioneer is Gloria Goldman, who writes about the use of simulated clinical experiences as an assessment tool in a two-year nursing program at Sinclair Community College. Goldman also addresses the important issues of reliability and validity in the faculty evaluations of nursing students' performance as they react to patient case studies.

Next to students in health science majors, those specializing in education may be the most intensely scrutinized via assessment. Karen Schmid and Susan Kiger tell us about the performance-assessment system that teacher-education programs in Indiana must develop in response to criteria established by the Indiana Professional Standards Board.

As Peter Ewell reminds us in the last article in this issue of *Collections*, most colleges and universities have shown little interest in interinstitutional comparisons. Thus the article by Roy Rodenhiser and Victoria Buchan about collaboration in assessment between two schools of social work describes a unique situation. In the piece by James Forest and Bruce Keith, both the institution—the U.S. Military Academy—and the comprehensive approach to engineering education and its assessment are also unique.

James McCambridge and Kathy Thornhill undertook a study of assessment in distance MBA programs. Responses to an on-line questionnaire for distance MBA providers revealed a wide range of assessment practices and much room for improvement in this arena.

Assessment in Disciplines Not Subject to Accreditation

Faculty in disciplines not subject to accreditation have often been the hardest to convince that outcomes assessment is an essential contributor to the improvement of teaching and learning. Nevertheless, there is much similarity across disciplines and types of academic institutions in the kinds of assessment instruments and methods employed. While the use of simulated patients may be uniquely applicable in health disciplines and senior design projects may be associated most readily with engineering education, measures of writing, oral presentations, case study analyses, and surveys of employers are ubiquitous across the spectrum of majors and institutions.

Barbara Fuhrmann gives us examples of the use of portfolios in history and surveys of entering and graduating urban studies and planning majors to assess growth in knowledge, skills, and attitudes. The urban studies and planning faculty devote a three-hour meeting to analyzing assessment findings, and graduating seniors contribute their own perspectives on the data during that session.

Billy Catchings describes a one-credit Web-based course for senior communication majors in which students develop portfolios and then jointly plan a presentation where their work is adjudicated by faculty. Physical education faculty Gwen Robbins, Debbie Powers, and Jerry Rushton have used a test of knowledge, an opinionnaire, a life-style questionnaire, and a series of tests for cardiorespiratory endurance to assess the effectiveness of a fitness/wellness course.

Virginia McKinley and Spencer McWilliams in one article, and Patricia Murphy in a second, illustrate assessment methods that can be applied in every discipline. According to McKinley and McWilliams, seniors at Warren Wilson College have for many years been required to write a letter assessing their college experiences in response to several guiding questions. Persistent comments in the senior letters have convinced faculty in environmental studies to strengthen a course in wilderness ecology that involves a one-month trip to a wilderness area and intercultural studies professors to require study abroad or another extended cross-cultural experience.

Outcomes assessment at the graduate level is particularly difficult since the curriculum in most majors is individualized and common learning outcomes generally are not specified. Thus Patricia Murphy's description of assessment in graduate programs at North Dakota State University is quite unusual. Faculty have agreed upon four common outcomes for graduate students and use rubrics to assess students' competence as demonstrated in term papers, course exams, theses, and oral presentations.

Standardized Measures of Student Learning in the Major

Readers may note that none of the articles selected thus far mentions the use of commercial or standardized tests in assessing student learning in the major. Graduates of programs in several professional fields must pass standardized tests for licensure or certification, and a few of these fields offer practice tests or exercises to help students prepare for those tests. The Educational Testing Service (ETS) offers tests in some fifteen majors (e.g., biology, history, and sociology), most of which are in fields not subject to accreditation. Where faculty agree that a standardized test provides a good match with the student learning outcomes they consider essential, the standardized tests provide the benefits of (1) being readily available, (2) possessing levels of reliability and validity that instructor-made tests may not attain without a lot of work, and (3) offering normative data against which the performance of local students may be compared.

Since standardized instruments must be administered in a time-constrained environment, they cannot cover all the aspects of college students' learning in a given major. Thus they must be supplemented by other measures designed or selected by departmental faculty. This issue of the *Collections* series provides a rich array of the kinds of measures faculty are developing and using in their own settings.

In the last article Peter Ewell explores the use and implications of standardized tests in teacher education. He notes that "the requirements for teacher certification and licensure differ markedly between states," then suggests that a consortium of states might "act together to align their standards, employ common tests, and report performance more consistently." The fact that such consortia have not been formed illustrates the pervasive resistance to comparing programs, institutions, and states in terms of college student learning. Most faculty and administrators believe that the diversity of opportunities provided across major fields, institutions, and states is one of the great strengths of higher education in the United States. But, as Ewell points out, the press to assess with a test that has swept over K–12 education in this country like a tidal wave is mounting among higher education's stakeholders. Only time will tell if the arguments for maintaining a diverse array of programs, curricula, learning outcomes, and assessment measures in our colleges and universities will prevail.

Faculty Development for Assessment

The Way to a Faculty Member's Head Is through the Discipline

Barbara D. Wright

Look for: Faculty development for colleagues in psychology, sociology, and political science. Learned societies in these fields provided ideas and support for presentations at a meeting of the New England Educational Assessment Network. From Assessment Update *17:3 (2005).*

Assessment gatherings have multiplied exponentially over the past fifteen years, and the amount of guidance now available through conferences, workshops, and other kinds of events is truly impressive. From the national organizations to accrediting agencies and statewide consortia to campus meetings and on-line resources, there are rich opportunities for postsecondary educators to learn about virtually all aspects of assessment: theory, practice, policy, methods, trends, costs, benefits, and so on.

Yet there is one aspect of assessment that has been neglected. Current offerings are overwhelmingly generic—that is, they do not speak specifically to the interests of a faculty member in sociology or geology, in art history or business. Yet the discipline is where a faculty member lives, literally and metaphorically. It is the discipline to which faculty members devote a lifetime of scholarship. It is love for and expertise in the discipline that they hope to cultivate in their students.

For years, when policymakers or administrators or others have complained that faculty are the chief obstacle to the implementation of assessment, I've wondered silently whether the complainers ever took the assessment conversation to those faculty members' home turf and spoke to them in their own language. I've always suspected that the assessment message would get through more readily if faculty were approached through their disciplines. In April 2004, my colleagues at the New England Educational Assessment Network (NEEAN) and I had an opportunity to test that theory.

Sponsorship

NEEAN was founded in 1995 by postsecondary educators in New England who wanted to provide their colleagues with opportunities to learn about best practices in assessment. As the assessment movement unfolded, NEEAN wanted to ensure that the energy devoted to assessment would actually improve student learning and strengthen institutional effectiveness.

Since its founding, NEEAN's signature event has been the Fall Forum. This one-day conference now offers nationally known keynote speakers and over a dozen sessions; it regularly attracts over three hundred participants from around the region. The Fall Forum has received excellent reviews over the years, but it too is a "generic" assessment event.

In fall 2003, NEEAN's advisory board members decided to try something different by reaching out to faculty who might not have been involved in assessment prior to that time by offering them a discipline-specific development opportunity. Thus began planning for a half-day spring workshop called Dialogues in the Disciplines. Thanks to the cooperation of the University of Massachusetts' Office of Assessment, we were able to hold the workshop in a central location, the Amherst campus. Our regional accrediting body, the New England Association of Schools and Colleges (NEASC), also supported this experiment. NEASC has an interest in extending awareness of assessment from the administrative to the faculty level; their collaboration was essential in getting publicity for our workshop to campuses and lending the event additional legitimacy.

Considerations

The first and most obvious decision to be made was which disciplines to focus on. We settled on a cluster of social sciences—psychology, sociology, and political science—for several reasons. First, these three represent popular disciplines that involve large numbers of faculty and students. In other words, we would have a significant pool of potential registrants—which was important, since for this first-time event we needed enough participation to break even financially—and a large pool of students who could eventually benefit from the use of assessment findings to improve learning and strengthen programs.

Second, we wanted the workshop and its three disciplinary tracks to have scholarly legitimacy with the social scientists that we hoped to serve. That meant looking to the learned societies, following their recommendations, and incorporating their materials into the three tracks. The American Sociological Association (ASA), the American Psychological Association (APA), and the American Political Science Association all had taken up the issue of assessment, had articulated positions on what constitutes good practice, and had posted discipline-specific materials on the Web. The ASA's initiatives had a particularly long history, and the APA had recently posted the findings of an assessment task force, including suggested learning goals for psychology majors and the suitability of a range of assessment methods for determining student achievement of the goals.

Third, we wanted the tracks to be led by faculty members in the three disciplines who had hands-on experience with assessment and who could speak with authority about defining learning goals, selecting assessment methods, using assessment findings, and avoiding pitfalls, specifically in terms of psychology, sociology, or political science. With the help of the learned societies and colleagues, we were fortunate to locate three excellent workshop leaders: Catherine Berheide of Skidmore

College in New York (sociology), Margaret Launius of Mansfield University in Pennsylvania, and John Ishiyama of Truman State University in Missouri (political science).

Fourth, it was important to us to put a local face on the workshop, so we paired our lead presenters with New England partners—faculty in the region who had assessment experience and would also bring some knowledge of our regional accrediting body's expectations, the local policy environment, and economic constraints. Steven Adair of Central Connecticut State University joined the sociology track; Donna Killian Duffy of Middlesex Community College in Massachusetts contributed to the psychology track; and Scott Erb of the University of Maine–Farmington rounded out the roster in the political science track. The lead presenters and New England partners were asked to plan their tracks together, and the collaborations worked very well.

Expectations for the Workshop

The workshop was scheduled for a Friday morning and opened with a thirty-minute plenary session, then the group split into the three discipline-based tracks for the next two hours, and finally, the full group convened for another half hour. The opening and closing plenaries were conceived as a chance to frame the questions and issues that participants might have in common.

The two-hour discipline-based portion of the morning was designed to be hands-on, interactive, and practical. In addition, the time with like-minded colleagues was intended to give participants the chance to talk in discipline-specific terms about issues such as appropriate learning goals, model assessment programs, traditions of the discipline, theoretical assumptions, the methods that flow from theory or tradition, and recommended resources.

It was important to NEEAN organizers that the tracks focus on more than just course-level assessment. We acknowledge the value of course-level assessment and its usefulness as an entry point for encouraging faculty interest in assessment. But at the same time, we wanted to challenge faculty to think beyond the limits of the individual courses they teach or their particular specialization. We wanted participants to ask questions about what their major *as a whole* adds up to and to consider cocurricular or off-campus experiences as well.

We stressed that the tracks, in addition to dealing with the assessment of cognitive knowledge, should address how to assess complex skills such as advanced writing or research or information literacy skills as well as values and dispositions. We feel strongly that if assessment does not include more ambitious outcomes, the movement leaves itself open to the charge that assessment is reductionist and trivializes higher learning. This does not mean that any discipline has developed fail-safe ways of assessing these less easily quantified goals, but we need to at least keep them on the table and keep trying to develop ways to promote and document them. By presenting more qualitative approaches such as portfolios, capstone projects, or performances, we hoped to give participants both some tools and some encouragement for tackling these most important but also most challenging learning outcomes.

Finally, we promised participants that they would hear about the possibilities for turning their work in assessment into conference presentations and publications and for connecting it with the scholarship of teaching and learning. We wanted participants to know, if they didn't realize it already, that assessment *can* be scholarly work and that it can be respected and rewarded like other scholarly work. As it happened, each of our tracks had a presenter with direct connections to the scholarship of teaching and learning, either through the Carnegie Foundation for the Advancement of Teaching or through a campus initiative.

What Worked?

The response to Dialogues in the Disciplines was very strong on two levels: first, in terms of registration and overall level of interest in the workshop, and, second, in terms of evaluation results.

Advertising for the April event began in late January and was carried out almost exclusively via e-mail. We eventually registered over 150 participants and actually had to turn faculty away from the most heavily enrolled track, psychology.

The role of the learned societies proved to be critical: they not only lent our enterprise legitimacy but also provided high-quality materials and helped us locate excellent presenters. In addition, they provided practical assistance, posting the workshop on their Web sites and assisting us with advertising. Two of them—the American Sociological Association and the American Psychological Association—even awarded us small faculty development grants to help defray expenses.

Judging from the evaluations, participants greatly enjoyed their time in the disciplinary tracks, talking about the specifics and making contacts with like-minded colleagues across campus boundaries. In regard to the level of the presentations, most participants said they learned useful things; only a handful felt that their assessment program was too advanced for them to benefit from the workshop. And the small number who came to argue against doing assessment at all seemed to enjoy that opportunity as well. Workshop participants were less enthusiastic about the plenary sessions.

What Next?

Flushed with the success of this first round of Dialogues in the Disciplines, NEEAN has decided to tackle assessment in the humanities. We plan to offer a second round of dialogues, this time with tracks for literature and culture studies, history, and philosophy and ethics. We anticipate that we'll be able to build on the things that worked in the first round, but we also recognize that the humanities present something of a challenge. Useful materials are not as readily available, and we may not find the same level of commitment to assessment in the relevant learned societies. But the next round presents a unique opportunity to shape discussion, stimulate new efforts, and move assessment of student learning forward on a very important front.

In 2005, Barbara D. Wright was assessment coordinator at Eastern Connecticut State University in Willimantic, Connecticut.

Assessment in the Major: Response to a State Initiative

Trudy W. Banta

Look for: Faculty taking charge of the campus response to a state mandate for assessment. Changes resulting from the process of instrument development as well as the interpretation of assessment findings are described. From Assessment Update 2:1 (1990).

Experience in working closely with faculty at institutions in Tennessee, Virginia, and New Jersey—here the early impetus for campus assessment originated in state coordinating agencies—leads me to conclude that faculty can take charge of assessment, using it to improve curricula and modes of instruction, even when they are initially spurred to act by an external request for evidence of accountability.

In 1979, Tennessee became the first state to allocate a portion of funding for higher education on the basis of evidence that institutions were collecting information about students' performance. Stimulated by the availability of "performance funding," faculty at the University of Tennessee, Knoxville (UTK), developed a systematic program of assessing achievement in both general education and the major field and of examining perceptions of program quality expressed in survey responses by enrolled students, dropouts, and alumni.

Since 1982, UTK faculty in 100 major fields have selected or developed comprehensive assessment activities for seniors, which are designed primarily to provide faculty with information about program effectiveness but also inform individual students about their levels of achievement.

While evaluative data derived from standardized exams have been somewhat helpful in curricular decision making, the *process* of developing their own assessment procedures has had a far greater impact on the faculty's thinking about academic programs and services at UTK. In considering how to construct an exit assessment experience, faculty have been encouraged to think together about the nature of the curriculum and the types of knowledge and skills students should derive from it. A portion of the resources provided by the provost to assist departments with instrument development has been spent to obtain the services of external consultants who have expertise in the disciplines. Considering these consultants' perspectives on departmental curricula has also been a formative activity for faculty.

As a result of the focus on common learning objectives for students, a focus that has been part of the process of developing outcomes assessment in the major, the following changes have occurred in a number of departments:

- Faculty have a stronger sense of shared purpose with respect to what graduates of their programs should know and be able to do.
- Several faculties have developed explicit statements of core objectives or competencies for students.
- Stronger agreement about curricular goals has led to increased consistency among faculty in the teaching of core courses.
- Faculty are now more likely to use statements of course objectives in organizing their teaching and to share these statements with students.
- A more orderly progression of courses from the lower to the upper division has been established, and upper-division courses are built more consciously on content that students have experienced in introductory courses.

The work on assessment instruments has stimulated interest in a variety of faculty-development activities. Departments have approached the UTK Learning Research Center to request assistance in writing measurable objectives for programs and courses, organizing course content according to sets of objectives, developing assignments and test items that tap reasoning and problem-solving skills, and constructing reliable assessments of performance. The faculty-development experiences that the center provides have enriched the environment for students' learning by improving the teaching skills of individual faculty.

Most of the assessment procedures developed by UTK faculty have utilized a multiple-choice, paper-and-pencil test as a basic component. In addition, however, many have incorporated essays or structured problems, and several have included a performance component. The latter procedures range from an in-basket exercise to a field-experience evaluation by field and faculty supervisors to the design of an ad campaign for a new product. In one of the humanities disciplines, the assessment procedure consists of a series of activities that take place over a full term in a senior capstone course and are evaluated by a faculty team. These activities include selecting a problem for an extended paper, identifying appropriate references, writing an outline and a first draft of the paper, completing the paper, and presenting it orally for critique by classmates. Initially, at least, final papers have been reviewed not only by UTK faculty but also by the external consultants who assisted in designing the assessment procedure and its related scoring criteria.

The foregoing paragraphs describe the effects—on curricula, instruction, and faculty development—of the process of constructing procedures for outcomes assessment in major fields. After administering these procedures to students, faculty have been stimulated to respond in additional ways—for example, by identifying program strengths and weaknesses that could be corrected in curriculum modifications made necessary by the change from a quarter-based to a semester calendar. Some faculties decided to require more core courses in their disciplines; others altered the nature of courses already in the core.

Individual instructors, influenced by students' failure to apply their knowledge to assessment activities, have increased opportunities for students to practice application skills in courses. Faculty have added field trips, internships, term projects, and problem-solving exercises in their classes and assignments. Instructors have also increased the proportion of items on classroom exams that call on such higher-order intellectual skills as application, analysis, synthesis, and evaluation.

UTK faculty have been typical, I believe, in their response to an assessment mandate that originated outside the institution. For a variety of reasons, most reactions were negative. In many departments, a negative faction remains, but in every department, those most concerned about teaching and students' learning took control of the assessment agenda and shaped it to serve important departmental purposes. Their activities increased the focus of most other departmental members on the purposes and means of education in the discipline and produced important changes in curricula and modes of instruction.

In 1990, Trudy W. Banta was professor of education and founding director of the Center for Assessment Research and Development at the University of Tennessee, Knoxville. She directed the campus assessment program at UTK.

Student Competence as a Basis for Assessment

Student Competence as the Basis for Designing Curricula, Instruction, and Assessment

Trudy W. Banta

Look for: Examples of mature competence-based education programs in a variety of disciplines at three universities. At two of the institutions, employers helped identify abilities essential for graduates to develop. At the third institution, students' electronic portfolios permit students to monitor their own progress and faculty to spot areas of program strength as well as areas that need improvement. From Assessment Update *14:1 (2002).*

Students, faculty, and employers benefit when a record of what students know and can do takes the place of time spent in class (credit hours) as the basis for describing student progress toward graduation. Students have a better sense of what is expected of them and what their learning adds up to as they pass carefully defined milestones in their academic programs. Faculty gain direction for instruction and assessment from statements about what students should know and be able to do. Transfer from one institution to another is easier when students carry with them evidence of their knowledge and skills levels. And the task of hiring and placing graduates becomes easier for employers when they can compare transcripts that describe candidates' curricular experiences and levels of achievement.

In an earlier editorial (Banta, 2001), I lamented the paucity of mature competence-based programs. Thus, it is a privilege to be able to present four articles related to competence-based education in this issue.

In the first article, Sharon Paranto (2002) describes how one department at Northern State University in South Dakota used five sources of data from stakeholders to identify areas of competence needed by graduates and then made changes in curriculum, instruction, and student services like job placement to ensure that program graduates would develop the specified skills and knowledge. For instance, when employers and alumni said the community needs "more civic-minded college graduates," faculty decided to encourage employers who sponsor internships for students to invite their interns to participate in service organizations and civic groups in which company employees are already engaged. In addition, service learning projects have been incorporated in more courses.

As they make the transition from a community college to a four-year institution, University of Arkansas at Fort Smith (UAFS) faculty are developing nine bachelor's degree programs that are competence-based and individualized. Some of the work involved in connection with three of these programs—nursing, manufacturing technology, and information technology—is described in the article by Sandi Sanders (2002). As at Northern State, employers have been involved in identifying the types and levels of skills and abilities that graduates of these programs should possess. Students in manufacturing technology complete a capstone project in which they function as a member of a team that is working with an employer to solve a real problem of interest to the employer. Students are evaluated as if they were actually employed by the company sponsoring their project.

UAFS programs are individualized, so that students can progress at their own pace, moving to a new level as they demonstrate competence in each specified outcome. In information technology, for instance, a student can obtain a certificate, an associate degree, or a baccalaureate degree as increasing levels of competence are determined through assessment.

Faculty at the University of Charleston in West Virginia arguably have attempted the most difficult task of all—agreeing on definitions of competence and levels of achievement for six liberal arts learning outcomes.

As at UAFS, students have individualized learning plans and can move ahead as they demonstrate competence at the required standard. Belcher, Malmberg, and Parkman (2002) tell us that technology is important to the success of their efforts: students' electronic portfolios allow faculty to examine the work of groups of students in order to spot potential areas of strength and weakness in the curriculum, and Datatel software gives students easy access to their transcript so that they can monitor their progress in competence attainment continually.

The UAFS and University of Charleston stories emphasize the importance of faculty collaboration and administrative leadership and support in implementing competence-based initiatives. On both campuses, an institution-wide assessment committee assists the effort by setting policy and providing faculty development experiences. In addition to periodic workshops on topics that faculty identify, UAFS uses a monthly assessment newsletter and an annual assessment fair to promote sharing of successful assessment strategies and to recognize those who are doing good work.

While the efforts of the aforementioned universities focus on the development of competence in undergraduates, a program called *Virtual U* takes us to a higher level of complexity (Moore and Williams, 2002). Virtual U can be used in developing the skills of the top campus administrators whose support is so vital to assessment. Virtual U allows players of the game to develop and test their competence in academic operations and faculty management, enrollment management, resource allocation and finance, physical plant activities, and performance indicators. Unfortunately, while Moore and William assign high marks for the extent to which it gives players opportunities to practice dealing with the financial aspects of managing an institution, they give low marks in the area of assessment. Virtual U's weakest point is not providing assessment data that would help players learn to document and improve student learning. We are still a long way from being able to remove that grade of Incomplete for measures of student learning on the State-by-State Report Card for Higher Education (National Center for Public Policy and Higher Education, 2000)!

References

Banta, T. "On Competence." *Assessment Update*, 2001, *13*(3), 3, 5, 10.

Belcher, A., Malmberg, M., and Parkman, A. "'Learning Your Way': Awarding Credits on the Basis of Competence." *Assessment Update*, 2002, *14*(1), 6–7, 15.

Moore, D., and Williams, K. "Virtual U." *Assessment Update*, 2002, *14*(1), 11, 15–16.

National Center for Public Policy and Higher Education. *Measuring Up 2000: The State-by-State Report Card for Higher Education*. National Center for Public Policy and Higher Education, 2000.

Paranto, S. "Assessing MIS Programs Using Feedback from and Partnerships with Business and Industry." *Assessment Update*, 2002, *14*(1), 1–2, 10.

Sanders, S. "Innovative Assessment for Innovative Learning at University of Arkansas Fort Smith." *Assessment Update*, 2002, *14*(1), 4–5, 10.

Agricultural Faculty Constructs Competence Matrix

Charles Cleland

Look for: Assessment in agricultural business utilizing a matrix that helps to locate where 17 areas of competence are addressed in the curriculum. The relative emphasis on each area revealed in the matrix determines the proportion of items in that area to be addressed in a faculty-developed comprehensive exam for seniors. From Assessment Update 2:2 (1990).

Charles Cleland and faculty colleagues in the agricultural business program at the University of Tennessee, Knoxville, have developed a matrix to assess congruence between course content and competence areas identified for undergraduate majors. Course titles are listed across the top of the matrix and 17 competence areas are listed on the left side. In the cells, each faculty member provides a rating between zero (none) and four (central) to indicate the emphasis given to each competence in the course(s) they teach. Cells containing ratings by multiple faculty are averaged, then ratings are totaled across all courses to obtain an estimate of the faculty's emphasis on each competence.

The proportion of questions for each competence area that appears on the faculty-developed comprehensive exam for seniors is related to the emphasis given the area in coursework. Student responses on the exam are categorized by competence area. Finally, faculty received a report of the percentage of items answered correctly in each of the 17 competence areas. This request has stimulated faculty discussion concerning (1) the importance of the competence areas, (2) the relative difficulty of exam items in each area, and (3) the match between expected competences of graduates and the learning opportunities offered within the agricultural business curriculum.

In 1990, Charles Cleland was professor of agriculture at the University of Tennessee, Knoxville.

Faculty Evaluation of Student Work: Simple, Powerful, and Overlooked

David A. Shupe

Look for: Use of a database containing agreed-upon learning outcomes and related rubrics to assess individual student learning. Data can be aggregated across students and courses to assess course, program, and institutional effectiveness. From Assessment Update *18:2 (2006).*

In their quest for good information on student learning outcomes, college and university faculty have consistently overlooked the day-to-day process by which they evaluate regular student coursework. This is understandable, for with the information systems they used to have, the only institutional data this process delivered were course grades, and course grades were correctly understood as lacking the clarity or specificity needed for organizational information about learning outcomes. Given this, faculty searched for other methods that would deliver the desired information. Faculty evaluation of student work in courses was disregarded, and this expedient approach was soon elevated to an axiomatic principle: assessment is not the same as evaluation.

In that context, this update from Minnesota (see "Re-Assessing Assessment," *Assessment Update* 13:5 [September–October 2001], pp. 6–7) delivers unexpected news: with small revisions and direct systems support, faculty evaluation of student work can easily deliver unprecedented quantities of well-organized multidimensional data on actual student achievement.

Using this approach, colleges and universities can become significantly better. Faculty can collectively set academic and professional standards for students that are maintained across the curriculum. Disciplinary faculty can know precisely the extent to which their students are demonstrating expected learning outcomes. Student advisers can compare precisely a student's actual achievements to date with the expected achievements in that student's chosen program. Colleges can continually have a picture of each student's readiness for the next learning opportunity. Institutional researchers can have a new wealth of data for investigating student learning. Students can receive a new college record that demonstrates what they know and can do. As students realize that this record can present their achievements to prospective employers, they will begin to care about what it shows. In short, colleges and universities will be able to distinguish themselves both by the demonstrated quality of their academic outcomes and by their ability, as organizations, to attend to the personal, professional, and intellectual development of their students.

All of this becomes feasible when administrators provide faculty with direct information systems support for the work they are already doing. This is not an advertisement for the software first used to do this any more than initial discussion of personal computers was an advertisement for the first company to make them. A barrier has been broken; what is feasible has now changed, and other software will surely follow. Here is how the process works:

1. *Faculty committees define the standards (desired student achievements and rubrics for their evaluation) for specific areas of achievement.* As differ-

ent faculty committees do this, an electronic library of standards (outcomes and rubrics) is developed over time; this library can be drawn on, as appropriate, throughout the institution. Fortunately, over the past ten years, much of this decision making has already been done by professional associations, programs, courses, and institutions as a whole. Those who have already done this have a tremendous head start over those who have not yet begun the journey.

This first definition stage takes seriously the language that is created by faculty. It also recognizes that evaluating student work according to precise qualitative standards rather than by numbers is the real cognitive shift in outcomes assessment and that this is done best when the focus is on overall student development—that is, defining what students should be able to demonstrate upon completion of their chosen academic programs.

2. *Faculty decide the settings and activities in which students will have an opportunity to demonstrate the defined expected achievements.* This comes in three variations, depending on how much is done by faculty committees and how much is done by individual instructors.

a. *Committees complete only step 1 above.* Individual instructors select, for their course sections, which committee-defined achievements and rubrics to attend to and decide which activities students will do that will become evidence for one or more of those achievements.

b. *The faculty committee takes an additional step, deciding which courses should address an area of achievement.* As participating instructors of these courses access the system record for the section taught, they are automatically presented with the defined achievements for that area. The instructors still decide which activities students will do and link each activity to one or more of the predefined achievements and rubrics.

c. *The faculty committee takes yet another step, defining not only the achievements and settings but also the activities that will constitute evidence of these achievements.* This becomes a "shared assessment," and thus all the assessment planning work has already been done for the individual instructor.

The flexibility of these three variations accommodates appropriately different situations within an institution or, indeed, even within a program and recognizes that which variation to use is best decided locally.

3. *Each course instructor evaluates each student's work using the defined achievements and criteria.* All of the prior decisions about achievements, rubrics, and activities have been incorporated into the electronic interface. Participating instructors attend to the student achievement in front of them, and this concludes the gathering of data on student learning outcomes.

There are several reasons why this process is preferable:

1. *This single process takes significantly less work than other ways of creating data.* While faculty judgment about standards and students is honored, all of the extra work typically associated with assessment activities—special assessment tests, portfolio reviews, end-of-term written reports for courses and programs—is eliminated. The standards are applied to work that each student is already doing and that each instructor is already evaluating.

2. *Excellent data on actual outcomes are generated from electronic files that link students to achievements, to settings, and to time periods.* General education outcomes can be extracted directly from the entire curriculum, including non–general education courses. The director of an academic program can see, for any completed academic term, the full set of all student outcomes from all participating courses. An academic program or institution can have aggregated data on actual student learning outcomes wherever and whenever faculty choose to pay attention. All students (and their advisors) can know how they are doing relative to the expected learning outcomes of all courses in which they are enrolled. More broadly, students (and their advisors) can know how they are doing relative to any set of expectations defined by the program or college. These results, taken together, fundamentally solve the challenge of learning outcomes data that has been such a struggle for the past two decades.

3. *When the newly available data on actual student achievements are fed back into the educational process, they have the potential, over time, of making the academic enterprise significantly stronger and better.* Immediately, the college or any academic program can have strong direct data wherever and whenever it chooses to apply this process. Depending on how broadly and consistently it applies this approach, it can have much more.

Accountability can be redefined in a way that works for the academic enterprise—that is, institutions are accountable for setting and applying clear standards; students are accountable for their individual results (Shupe, 2002). Academic standards can be maintained across the curriculum. The institution can continually have a picture of any student's readiness for the next learning opportunity. Likewise, it is possible to evaluate the readiness of any set of students—whether in prospect (those who are enrolling for a specific course) or in retrospect (those who have participated in a learning community or other shared experience). The institution and any of its programs can be distinctive both in expected outcomes and in actual outcomes.

It will take time for colleges to take advantage of this approach. A number of them are already beginning to do so. Rochester Community and Technical College in Minnesota was the first to begin and is progressively applying this process to a variety of academic programs. Kirkwood Community College in Iowa has begun by applying this approach to developmental education. Anoka Ramsey Community College in Minnesota is using it to document outcomes in general education. Quinebaug Valley Community College in Connecticut, in part because it is small, is applying it to the widest range of outcomes. However, this process is not limited to community colleges; for example, Concordia University in Minnesota has begun to use the approach as well.

Underwriting what students and faculty are already doing is both simple and powerful, and it is clear that over time, it can produce all of these unprecedented results. In the future, as we look back, perhaps we will see how pervasive and how pernicious was the invisibility of educational results to which we all had been so accustomed.

Reference

Shupe, D. "Envisioning a Thoroughly Academic Accountability and a Thoroughly Accountable Academy." Paper presented at the annual conference of the North Central Association Higher Learning Commission, Chicago, Mar. 2002.

In 2006, David A. Shupe was director of evaluation of student achievement for eLumen Collaborative, an independent academic research and development firm in St. Paul, Minnesota.

Assessment in Disciplines Subject to Accreditation

Simulated Performance Assessment in a Community College Nursing Program

Gloria Goldman

Look for: Performance assessment in nursing using patient actors and computer simulations, based on case studies. Predictive validity and inter-rater reliability for faculty observers of students' responses to case material are addressed. From Assessment Update 11:3 (1999).

The nursing faculty of Sinclair Community College are making significant changes in curriculum and in student learning activities designed to operationalize the curriculum. These changes are based in part on data collected over three years of measuring student learning outcomes using the Structured Simulated Clinical Examination (SSCE). Outcomes data compiled from the performance assessment of more than two hundred students were used to identify strengths and weaknesses of the program and to plan modifications of course content and student learning experiences.

The importance of performance assessment in applied practice disciplines cannot be overemphasized. All health professions require practitioners to demonstrate certain standards of clinical competence in order to protect the public, ensure quality of services, and establish the credibility of their members (Coates and Chambers, 1992). For this reason, a great deal of attention has historically been devoted to performance assessment in nursing. Nurse educators have long espoused what other educators are recently suggesting: that what matters is how students use knowledge, not just whether they possess requisite knowledge. There are important learning objectives that cannot be adequately assessed by paper-and-pencil tests.

Assessment of learning outcomes in nursing traditionally takes place in clinical areas as students provide care to patients. While clinical evaluation of student performance is one of the most important aspects of the teaching-learning process, it is also one of the most difficult. Multiple, complex problems exist with any attempt to assess student performance in clinical settings—the subjectivity of judgments made by faculty, constraints on the number of individual student behaviors that can be assessed, the variation of student assignments, and the changing nature of clinical settings, to name but a few.

To overcome some of the problems inherent in basing decisions about curriculum and instruction on data derived from paper-and-pencil tests and clinical evaluation, some nursing programs have moved to performance examinations (McKnight and others, 1987; Johnson, Lehman, and Sandoval, 1988; Ross and others, 1988; Bujack, McMillan, Dwyer, and Hazelton, 1991; Lenburg and Mitchell, 1991). The nursing faculty of Sinclair Community College have developed a performance assessment methodology using simulated clinical settings and patient problems. The SSCE, a highly modified version of the Objective Structured Clinical Examination (OSCE) used in many schools of medicine, provides a systematic means of assessing each student's mastery of complex, integrated skills in the affective, cognitive, and psychomotor domains. This performance examination uses a case study format, patient-actors, and observation of student performance by faculty raters using standardized rating scales.

The case study is a written simulation that describes the patient, the patient's presenting problem or problems, any medical and nursing interventions already being implemented, and information needed to plan a response. Students are required to seek additional information and to act as if they were in the actual clinical area. The case study becomes a scenario, sequencing the patient's responses to the student and requiring the student to engage in problem solving. It is essential that each case study provide for assessment of a sample of behaviors that represent the overall performance of each student. The key to using case studies is the assumption that a student's response or course of action in relation to an exemplary case can be generalized to all cases (Priestly, 1982).

To allow for utilization of a wide variety of case studies while maintaining an acceptable level of control, the faculty created a model to facilitate standardization of rating scale development. Development of rating scales using this carefully constructed model based on professional standards ensures a high degree of consistency. Content and construct validity of the model for rating scale development were established through incorporating professional standards and utilizing feedback from faculty subject-matter experts and twenty-five clinical nurse managers employed in five area hospitals. Messick (1989) has asserted that content validity is based on professional judgments about the relevance of the content of the examination to the content of a particular domain and about the representativeness with which the content covers that domain. Consensual expert judgment is an important part of ensuring content and format relevance.

Faculty raters are selected and trained as a group using a detailed training manual and a twenty-minute video produced in the college's television studio. According to Thorndike and others (1991), although training sessions will not eliminate all shortcomings of the rating process, they do reduce the more common distortions. Following rater training, patient-actors are oriented to their roles. Brief written scripts are shared with these individuals (students from the Theater Department, nursing students not being tested, and staff members) and short practice sessions are held. The use of actual hospital equipment and supplies enhances the authenticity of the testing environment. Following each examination session, debriefing sessions are held with students and faculty raters and actors. Information from these sessions has been useful in continually improving the examination process.

Faculty assumptions that careful rater and actor training, attention to the authenticity of the testing environment, and ongoing incorporation of suggestions for improvement contribute to validity and reliability of the SSCE have been affirmed. A study of inter-rater reliability was conducted with a sample of forty-seven students tested by six pairs of faculty raters. Mean scores indicated a confirming level of agreement by raters at all stations, and all intraclass and interclass correlations were significant at $p = 0.0001$. A study of predictive validity designed to compare performance on the SSCE of forty-eight students at the end of the program with performance of these same individuals during the first year of clinical practice as registered nurses was also conducted. Correlation coefficients ranged from .00 to .29, and there were no statistically significant relationships between criterion and predictor variables at the .05 alpha level. However, there were positive relationships between most criteria and there were no negative relationships. In addition, data analysis strengthened the claim of content and construct validity, and valuable information about employer expectations was obtained.

Faculty were appropriately hesitant to make changes in curriculum and teaching methodologies in response to assessment findings until validity and reliability of the SSCE could be established. Inferences about students' abilities to apply knowledge in real-life situations, and faculty decisions and actions based on those inferences, should certainly be made using the most valid and reliable information available. Once the faculty could be sure that the SSCE possesses an acceptable level of validity and reliability, they were able to use assessment findings with confidence.

Perhaps the most valuable data obtained through use of the SSCE to date have to do with the poor performance of students in cognitive areas related to clinical decision making. Follow-up efforts revealed that students perceive themselves as not engaged in decision making while in the actual clinical practice setting. They are more likely to collect information and pass it on to the clinical staff or faculty than to make decisions and have them validated. Many students cited lack of personal confidence in their abilities to make sound decisions and low expectations of them by faculty and clinical staff as primary reasons for their hesitation.

Faculty immediately responded to this finding by proactively addressing the importance of critical thinking and clinical decision-making skill development and by promoting active decision making by students in the clinical area. A significant curriculum revision has been initiated, with learning opportunities for critical thinking and decision making embedded in each nursing course. Faculty development efforts have been successful in improving the skills of individual faculty in facilitating student thinking and decision making.

A recently acquired computerized Human Patient Simulator will allow nursing faculty to move to a new level of sophistication in utilizing the SSCE. Case studies are programmed into the computer and run automatically, causing the simulator to respond in completely predictable and realistic ways to each student intervention and obviating the need for actor training. Invasive procedures that cannot be performed on patient-actors will be possible with the simulator, allowing the practice and assessment of highly complex and potentially risky interventions to be performed safely.

Although the SSCE will never completely replace paper-and-pencil tests and clinical evaluation as assessment methodologies, it does provide a valuable means of assessing student learning outcomes in authentic settings. This performance examination allows faculty to maintain high ecological validity while eliminating the extraneous variables found in actual clinical settings. At Sinclair Community College, the SSCE has enabled faculty, with a high degree of confidence, to create changes in what and how students are learning. We believe that these changes will result in immediate enhancement of student learning and in continuous institutional improvement.

References

American Assembly of Collegiate Schools of Business, *Achieving Quality and Continuous Improvement through Self-Evaluation and Peer Review: Standards for Accreditation, 1994–1995.* St. Louis, MO: American Assembly of Collegiate Schools of Business, 1994.

Bujack, L., McMillan, M., Dwyer, J., and Hazelton, M. "Assessing Comprehensive Nursing Performance—The Objective Structured Performance Assessment (OSPA), Part One: Development of the Assessment Strategy." *Nursing Education Today*, 1991, *11*(3), 179–184.

Coates, V., and Chambers, M. "Evaluation Tools to Assess Clinical Competence." Nursing Education Today, 1992, 12, 122–129.

Johnson, G., Lehman, B., and Sandoval, J. "Clinical Exam: A Summative Evaluation Tool." *Journal of Nursing Education*, 1988, 27, 373– 374.

Lenburg, C., and Mitchell, C. "Assessment of Outcomes: The Design and Use of Real Simulation Nursing Performance Examinations." *Nursing and Health Care*, 1991, 12, 68–74.

McKnight, J., Rideout, E., Brown, B., Ciliska, D., Rankin, J., and Woodward, C. "The Objective Structured Clinical Examination: An Alternative Approach to Assessing Student Clinical Competence." *Journal of Nursing Education*, 1987, 26, 39–41.

Messick, S. "Validity." In R. Linn (Ed.), *Educational Measurement*. New York: American Council on Education, 1989.

Priestly, M. *Performance Assessment in Education and Training: Alternative Techniques.* Englewood Cliffs, NJ: Education Technology Publications, 1982.

Ross, M., Carroll, G., Knight, J., Chamberlain, M., Fothergill-Bourbannais, F., and Linton, J. "Using the OSCE to Measure Clinical Skills Performance in Nursing." *Journal of Advanced Nursing*, 1988, 13, 45–58.

Thorndike, R. M., Cunningham, G. K., Thorndike, R. L., and Hagen, E. P. *Measurement and Evaluation in Psychology and Education*. Old Tappan, NJ: Macmillan, 1991.

In 1999, Gloria Goldman was chair of the Nursing Department at Sinclair Community College.

Competence-Based Curricula and Assessment: The Case of Teacher Education in Indiana

Karen Schmid, Susan J. Kiger

Look for: Lessons learned about assessing student performance across the curriculum using a state standards-based example from teacher education. The importance of developing collaboration in assessment across disciplines is emphasized. From Assessment Update *15:1 (2003).*

The state of Indiana mandated a competence-based system for the preparation and licensure of educators, effective July 1, 2002. This requires teacher preparation programs to infuse standards throughout the curriculum and to put in place a coherent, sequential assessment system for individual students that includes performance assessments. Indiana's new system has been characterized as being in the national forefront (Scannell and Metcalf, 2000). If this is the case, describing the experience of Indiana State University (ISU) may prove helpful to other colleges and universities. More than 2,700 students are majoring in programs that lead to initial teacher licensure at ISU, so this is a large project. The focus of this article is the education of beginning teachers.

Background

Indiana's new system for teacher education is standards-driven and performance-based. It is complex, responding to multiple sets of standards. Standards "may be seen as another term for outcomes or competences" (Dietz, 2001, p. 36), so "competence-based" is substituted at times for other language used in the Indiana framework. The standards of the Interstate New Teacher Assessment and Support Consortium (INTASC) furnish the basis for all of Indiana's standards. National standards of learned societies and organizations provided direction for the development of state content standards. In addition, the National Council for the Accreditation of Teacher Education (NCATE) has a new set of standards that are consistent with Indiana's system.

To be recommended for initial teacher licensure, students must meet sets of standards for the developmental level and content area of licensure sought. Each developmental level—early childhood, middle childhood, early adolescence, and adolescence/young adulthood—has its own set of seven to nine standards. In addition, licensure must be sought in a specific content area or areas. Besides the developmental standards, each content area has its own set of standards, most often ten in number, each having a corresponding delineation of knowledge, disposition, and performance statements used to meet the standard.

All sets of standards in the Indiana system are performance-based, meaning that achievement of any particular standard is documented through demonstration of the knowledge, skills, or dispositions, or sets of those, associated with successful performance of the standards. For example, mathematics standard #1 is "Teachers of mathematics understand the key concepts and procedures of mathematics and have a broad understanding of the mathematics curriculum. Teachers of mathematics understand the appropriate structures within the discipline and its interaction with technology." A student's demonstration of reaching an acceptable level on this standard might be documented by relatively succinct performances, such as passing course examinations and writing papers, or by very complex performances such as teaching a unit in a field experience.

While the Indiana Professional Standards Board (IPSB), the state agency responsible for governing teacher preparation and licensure, specifies that the teacher education institution must account for achievement of all the standards for any particular license, the institution decides on the curriculum and assessments by which this will be accomplished. Given the possible combinations of sets of standards for the number of licenses any institution may offer, and the requirement for performance assessments for each standard within the combination of sets, the complexity becomes apparent.

To keep track of all this, the IPSB requires each college or university that has a teacher education program to develop a Unit Assessment System (UAS), which documents the curricula and assessments of teacher education students. The UAS must include a coherent, sequential assessment system for each individual student who is seeking licensure, to document whether he or she has demonstrated successful achievement of the standards or where each student is developmentally in terms of that achievement. In addition, the UAS must be constructed in such a fashion that all the collected data may be aggregated to provide information about the overall quality of each teacher education program. The state provided criteria and a rubric to guide both the development and ongoing review and revision of the assessment system.

Indiana State University's Experience

ISU's experience illustrates some of the challenges of implementing a competence-based system. First among the challenges was the increased collaboration of units across campus that was necessary to make decisions and to conceptualize and implement the performance assessments. As a result of many meetings, it became clear that, unlike the previous licensing requirements, the standards are independent of any class or number of credits, which precipitated an interesting dialogue. Some faculty interpreted this to mean that performance assessments should be separate from classes. But most universities are organized around classes and credit hours, and as the realities of the new system became clear, faculty decided to embed most assessments in classes.

Faculty faced a second challenge as they engaged in extensive curriculum mapping to specify in which classes given standards were addressed and assessed. Faculty collaboratively decided that if a student earns a "C" or better in a class that specifically addresses a standard or subset of the standards, this signifies that the student has performed at an acceptable level on the assessment and the standard.

Each department created syllabi for the courses in which performances are assessed. These syllabi articulate the learning activities by which students demonstrate competence and document the grading system as reflective of particular levels of achievement. In addition, each department is responsible for keeping artifacts that exemplify "A" through "F" work on assessments, to document the relationship between grades and meeting standards for the UAS and outside evaluators from IPSB and NCATE. Each department determined the data to be collected for and reported to the UAS database from each of the designated courses. Finally, entire programs were collaboratively reviewed to ensure coverage of all standards and proper reporting and, most important, to ensure that our approach was developmental, with multiple assessment opportunities for students to demonstrate competence.

In developing syllabi and specific learning activities, we spent substantial time exploring the notion of performance assessment. Initially, many faculty thought that performance assessment required specification of numerous discrete tasks and checklists—perhaps even hundreds of them—similar to the competence-based approach of the 1970s. Over time, and as a result of numerous internal meetings and meetings sponsored collaboratively by the School of Education, the various professional schools, and the College of Arts and Sciences, it became clear that summative assignments, in which faculty could assess performance on more than one standard, would prove efficacious.

For example, complex learning activities such as the teaching that occurs in field experiences demonstrate competence pertaining to a number of developmental and content standards simultaneously. We have developed rubrics to ensure accurate, reliable assessment by both university faculty and the K–12 teachers who supervise university students in field experiences. These assessments inform not only the instructor of the course in which the field experience is housed but also the education program and school or college in which the student's major is housed. However, the multiple-item checklist approach still proves valid and useful for some courses, depending on the nature of the standards targeted for assessment. We have come to appreciate varied approaches to assessment.

Lessons Learned and Continuing Challenges

Implementation of a competence-based system of this size and complexity is costly in time and resources. An enormous amount of faculty and administrative time over six years has gone into development of the system, course revision and creation, program updating, revision of the catalogue and other publications, creation of performance assessments, development of numerous record-keeping and storage systems, stakeholder involvement, and informing students. This has taken significant time away from scholarly activities, service to the community, contributing to other university priorities, and many other needed and desirable activities. The picture is not entirely bleak, however, for we have learned a number of important lessons and gained a clearer vision of the forthcoming challenges.

An obvious recommendation for those considering development of competence-based curricula and assessments is to reduce complexity. The multiple, overlapping sets and permutations of standards that Indiana requires could be collapsed into one or two well-articulated sets. While we did not do this from the outset, as we moved into development of our performance assessments and UAS, those connections became clear. Those beginning this process would be well advised to clarify connections first.

A benefit is that what we have learned about assessment for teacher education has increased the knowledge base about assessment in general; after all, performance assessment does not pertain only to teacher education. Unfortunately, the impact has been less widespread than it could have been, because many faculty who teach subject matter courses see the standards and assessments as overly bureaucratic. As the system becomes more established and if there are clear benefits, perhaps the jargon, rules, and regulations will not seem as remote and onerous as they currently do to many faculty.

Through our mutual struggle to understand and programmatically articulate coherent teacher education, we have come to know and appreciate each other's strengths as faculty and scholars. Our collaborative skills have increased, because we must cooperate across the many units in-volved in teacher education: 16 departments housed in four professional schools and the College of Arts and Sciences. Palomba (2001) indicates the critical importance of collaboration in ensuring successful assessment across the number of units involved in professional programs. Moreover, this benefit will be of particular importance as the unit undergoes IPSB and NCATE accreditation reviews.

Many challenges remain. Competence-based programs theoretically facilitate transfer of students between colleges and universities (Banta, 2002). This is not necessarily true in practice. Indiana teacher licensure standards are identical across the state, but different colleges and uni-versities structure curricula and assessments differently. Other states have different standards. Departments must prepare alternate ways for trans-fer students to demonstrate that they have met standards that are em-bedded in ISU courses. Unless definitions of competence are standardized across the United States, competence-based systems are likely to make transfer of students from one university to another more time-consuming and difficult. On the other hand, change of major within the university is facilitated by embedding standards in courses and using grades to signify that students have performed adequately.

One concern is whether we will be able to make sense of all the data that will be collected through the UAS. While we are working from models that have been proven for teacher education applications and we have searched diligently for the most adaptable database, the proof will lie in our ability to refine the system according to our developing under-standing of information needs. Indeed, we are not sure we are asking *all* the right questions yet.

Ultimately, the point is whether it is worth it. Will all of this effort to develop a competence-based system for teacher education lead to better preparation of teachers and, consequently, improvement in K–12 student learning and performance? At this time, the payoff looks promising, but it is uncertain. Initial data from early stages of implementation of the new system indicate an increase in the performance levels of our preservice teachers in early field experiences and student teaching. The data also document an increase in their ability to reflect and propose appropriate changes in a unit that they have taught.

Finally, we come full circle to the big questions that began the whole standards-driven, performance-based system. Will societal and political concerns about education be satisfied? Will this provide sufficient accountability? Is this the most effective and efficient way to improve the education of children? We have no answers yet.

References

Banta, T. W. "Student Competence as the Basis for Designing Curricula, Instruction, and Assessment." *Assessment Update*, 2002, *14*(1), 3, 15.

Dietz, M. E. "Assessing Student Competence in Teacher Education Programs." In C. A. Palomba and T. W. Banta (eds.), *Assessing Student Competence in Accredited Disciplines*. Sterling, VA: Stylus, 2001.

Palomba, C. A. "Assessment Experiences in Accredited Disciplines." In C. A. Palomba and T. W. Banta (eds.), *Assessing Student Competence in Accredited Disciplines*. Sterling, VA: Stylus, 2001.

Scannell, M. M., and Metcalf, P. L. "Autonomous Boards and Standards-Based Teacher Development." *Educational Policy*, 2000, 14, 61–76.

In 2003, Karen Schmid was interim associate vice president for academic affairs and Susan J. Kiger was assistant professor, Department of Curriculum, Instruction, and Media Technology in the School of Education at Indiana State University.

Outcomes Assessment: Collaboration between Schools of Social Work

Roy W. Rodenhiser, Victoria Buchan

Look for: Collaboration in assessment by faculty at two institutions offering majors in social work. Use of the same assessment instruments at two universities permits comparisons that may provide faculty with additional motivation to undertake program improvements. From Assessment Update 8:1 (1996).

Assessment of social work programs at the University of North Dakota (UND) and Colorado State University (CSU) is a unique and collaborative venture. The two schools of social work have sought to test a model of program monitoring developed by one and enhanced by the other. This cooperative approach to program assessment has proved to be a boon to both programs.

An internal evaluation perspective is the basis for the approach used by UND and CSU. It represents a value principle that assessment should focus on curriculum content, the student learning process, and the usefulness of that learning content and experience beyond the university environment. We believe that students are the primary consumers of the educational "product" and that, logically, they are among those best suited to evaluate its success or failure. The internal evaluation perspective is more concerned with the actual impact of the educational process on the student.

Program Monitoring

The assessment method used by both schools is called Program Monitoring, which is defined as continual or longitudinal program evaluation. These days it usually includes the use of a data base program or management information system. The software chosen to maintain the data was R-Base 5000 (Erickson and Kroenke, 1985), which has been upgraded twice to R-Base 3.1.

The objective of Program Monitoring is program management. Data input is continual, and programmatic adjustments can be implemented before problems become unmanageable or entrenched. Consistent feedback allows programs to look for trends, anticipate needs, and continually monitor the target population.

Instrument Development and Assessment at CSU

Instrument development and data collection began at CSU with bachelor of social work (B.S.W.) exit surveys in 1985-1986. Based on this first attempt, a number of changes were made in the survey instrument. All instruments include both quantitative and qualitative data. The instruments used by both schools include entry data forms, exit interview forms, follow-up interview forms, and employer evaluation forms. Currently in the planning stage is development of a short version of the field supervisor's final evaluation for both levels of students. The data collected by CSU and UND focus on (1) students' perceptions of their knowledge, skills, professional development, and field experience at the time of their graduation; (2) students' perceptions of their knowledge, skills, and professional development two years after they have graduated; and (3) employers' perceptions of the graduates' knowledge, skills, and professional development two years after they have graduated.

The knowledge areas tap typical social work curriculum issues such as knowledge of human behavior, social welfare, practice, and research. The skills area includes common social work interviewing and problem-solving techniques. The professional development area assesses key ethical and values criteria. In addition, general demographic data are collected.

Cumulative reports are run at the end of each school year and put into tabular and narrative format. Basic content analysis is utilized on the open-ended questions, and frequencies within thematic categories are given. Individual statements related to specific curriculum or department issues are also included.

Assessment at UND

The comprehensive UND Social Work Assessment Plan was developed and adopted by the faculty in spring 1992. UND began collecting data in summer 1992 using the modified CSU instruments. So far, exit interview data have been collected for four M.S.W. graduating classes and three B.S.W. graduating classes. Cumulative reports are run at the end of each year and put into a format similar to CSU's.

Regular reports of ongoing assessments are shared with key department administrative personnel and committees. For example, evaluations regarding curriculum outcomes are regularly communicated to the Curriculum Committee for purposes of curriculum enhancement and standards accountability. Formative information regarding student perspectives is communicated to department administrative team members and the faculty as a whole for program modification.

Faculty Collaboration

The researchers identify discussion areas to be shared between the two faculties for program evaluation and enhancement. For example, students' perceptions of their field experiences and the evaluation scores of the field supervisors from both schools were compared. Discussion between the two faculties about the differences that were found led to program improvements at both schools.

Another area of collaboration involves the curriculum. Both CSU and UND function in rural environments. Sharing knowledge about differences (or similarities) in curricula assists both institutions in improving the quality of curriculum delivery. By reviewing assessment results longitudinally, we can manage change more effectively to ensure that we are conforming to accreditation guidelines and maintaining the integrity of our programs.

Faculty can work together on special projects related to accreditation and the delivery of a professional curriculum. By sharing assessment data, the two faculties look at many special issues, such as ethnicity, rurality, and aging, from a broader perspective. Other special issues include the impact of adding a new graduate program to a concurrently offered undergraduate program (both UND and CSU share this history) and evaluating the placement of graduates as it relates to relevant training.

The collaboration effort has been successful and rewarding to this point and the potential for enhancing program delivery and faculty learning is very strong. In addition, success with the model at one school appears to indicate reliability for some or all of the instruments used at the other school, and the input from one faculty is invaluable in helping to determine what works and what needs changing in the other school's programs. We have found that our faculties are much more re-sponsive to feedback because comparative data between the two schools were available.

Interesting patterns are beginning to emerge and merit further study. For instance, there appears to have been a regression to the mean for both programs at the M.S.W. level from the euphoria of finally establishing master's programs, to the reality of clear student feedback on program deficiencies.

Conclusion

Schools of social work have, for many years, responded to accreditation standards set by the Council on Social Work Education. Increasingly, colleges, universities, and various state commissions are adding to department workloads by continually requesting evaluation feedback.

The model of Program Monitoring developed by CSU and adapted and improved by UND is based on a belief that student performance constitutes an accurate source of curriculum and program feedback. The potential for sharing data and enhancing both programs is just beginning to be realized. We hope that other institutions will become interested in joining this collaborative effort. Each additional school enhances the potential for increasing educational effectiveness.

Reference

Erickson, W., and Kroenke, D. R-Base 5000. Bellevue, WA: Microrim, 1985.

In 1996, Roy W. Rodenhiser was assistant professor in the School of Social Work at the University of North Dakota, Grand Forks, and Victoria Buchan was associate professor in the School of Social Work at Colorado State University, Fort Collins.

Assessing Proficiency in Engineering and Technology within a Multidisciplinary Curriculum

James JF Forest, Bruce Keith

Look for: Detailed definitions of desired learning outcomes in engineering and technology and descriptions of multiple sources of assessment data, including students' course products and opinions and the views of graduates and employers. From Assessment Update 16:4 (2004).

The United States Military Academy (USMA) provides cadets with the intellectual foundation that they will need to succeed as military officers. The abilities to shape the physical world and to lead others in doing so are important competences of an Army officer. Therefore, the study of engineering and technology is fundamental to the education of cadets at West Point and embodies an important goal of the Military Academy's academic program.

The Learning Model

The overarching goal of the USMA's academic program is for graduates to anticipate and respond effectively to the uncertainties of a changing technological, social, political, and economic world. This goal demands that our graduates be effective problem solvers. The study of engineering develops a specialized form of problem solving—one that uses mathematics, science, and technology as tools—and is reflected in the USMA's engineering and technology goal. West Point's general education curriculum exposes cadets early in their experience to a common model for the engineering design process that forms a conceptual framework for the study of all engineering science and engineering design concepts taught at the Military Academy.

The engineering design process is described as a cycle consisting of four major phases: problem definition, design and analysis, decision making, and implementation. All four phases are performed within a problem-solving environment constrained by technological, economic, political, and social considerations. All four phases are oriented toward achieving the desired end state: a system, component, or process that meets a human need. Each of the four major phases is itself a cycle—a characteristic that underscores the iterative nature of engineering design. Once this framework is understood, key engineering concepts can be learned in the context of their potential application in problem solving. This framework forms a comprehensive learning structure for developing cadets' engineering and technological proficiency.

The Military Academy enables cadets to achieve the engineering and technology goal via one of two paths. While achievement of this goal is most evident among cadets majoring in any of our programs that are accredited by the Accreditation Board for Engineering and Technology (ABET/CSAB), the core curriculum at West Point includes several mathematics and basic science courses, and a three-course engineering sequence is required for all non-engineering majors. During their first two years, cadets learn the fundamental principles on which engineering applications are based. Core courses also facilitate the subsequent study of engineering by enhancing cadets' quantitative problem-solving skills and by providing introductory engineering design experiences.

Building on this foundation, cadets take one of several available three-course core engineering sequences. Each sequence is structured to provide breadth and depth in a selected engineering discipline and features an early exposure to an engineering design process, a well-integrated progression from predominantly engineering science to predominantly engineering design, and a culminating design project. This project provides cadets with an opportunity to synthesize and apply concepts from previous courses and to demonstrate substantial achievement of the engineering and technology goal. The engineering design requirement also reinforces cadets' achievement of other academic program goals, including the development of creativity and communication skills.

Outcomes Assessment

The Engineering and Technology Goal Team, a multidisciplinary group of faculty, maintains principal ownership of the design and assessment of this goal. The team's work is supported and reviewed by faculty through the Assessment Steering Committee, the Curriculum Committee, and the dean. To measure cadets' achievement of the engineering and technology goal effectively, this goal team has articulated the standards of performance that we expect cadets to achieve.

Our assessment initiatives seek to determine the extent to which graduates have reached this standard. These efforts include an evaluation of cadets' ability to (1) demonstrate basic-level technical proficiency in an engineering discipline that is relevant to the needs of the Army; (2) define a complex technological problem, accounting for its political, social, and economic dimensions; (3) determine what information is required to solve a technological problem, acquire that information from appropriate sources, and formulate reasonable assumptions that facilitate a solution; (4) apply the engineering design process and use appropriate technology to develop solutions that are both effective and adaptable; (5) demonstrate creativity in the formulation of alternative solutions to a technological problem; (6) plan the implementation of an engineered solution; (7) communicate that solution to both technical and nontechnical audiences; and (8) assess the effectiveness of an engineered solution. As is reflected in these competence goals for West Point graduates, our approach to the development of cadets' engineering and technological proficiency necessitates a broad, multidisciplinary perspective.

Our assessment of the engineering and technology goal involves triangulation of data, including an analysis of surveys, student course products, and employer feedback. Our review of longitudinal survey data reveals that cadets' confidence in their own engineering and technological proficiency increases significantly during their four-year experience at West Point, particularly when asked to describe their ability to use available math, science, and other tools to solve basic real-world technical problems and to employ the Army's new technology.

Additional assessment evidence is provided by content analyses of essays, research papers, formal presentations, and other course products, including the design project required at the end of the three-course core engineering sequence. Surveys administered to USMA graduates and their employers (typically unit field commanders) consistently reveal that both the graduates and their commanders are confident in our graduates' abilities to "solve basic real-world engineering problems." These views are further substantiated by the assessment evidence we gather through focus group interviews of former battalion commanders at the Army War College—that is, evaluations from upper-level management.

USMA faculty have spent the past several years working through an iterative process to assess cadets' achievement of the engineering and technology goal. Our analysis of the assessment data gathered through these activities indicates that USMA graduates perform very well on this dimension of the academic program. Furthermore, we are convinced that these efforts are yielding positive results, both in terms of improving our curriculum and moving the USMA toward an academic culture of renewal through long-term assessment. Nonetheless, we have not and perhaps will not reach an end state; we are learning valuable lessons as we move forward with this initiative. Annual analyses of the data have led us to revise questionnaire items and the overall assessment process. Perhaps one of the most important lessons learned thus far is that assessment is a process—a continual cycle of gathering information, assessing it, examining the methodological issues, refining the instruments, and then gathering more information. In addition, we have learned the importance of gathering evidence annually from multiple sources, including cadets' course work and opinions as well as the views of graduates and employers.

Conclusion

West Point equips graduates with the technical problem-solving skills that are necessary for effective leadership as military officers. The assessment data we have gathered to date suggests that USMA cadets and graduates generally achieve the standard set by the Engineering and Technology Goal Team. We find that directing our attention to a comprehensive assessment process directed by multidisciplinary goals and teams of faculty is producing qualitative change in our academic program and curriculum.

In 2004, James JF Forest was assistant professor of political science and assistant dean for academic assessment, and Bruce Keith was professor and associate dean for academic affairs at the United States Military Academy, West Point, New York.

Assessment Practices for Distance MBA Programs: A Snapshot

James A. McCambridge, Kathy L. Thornhill

Look for: Findings from a national survey of providers of distance MBAs regarding their assessment practices. There is little agreement on what to assess or how to do it. From Assessment Update 17:1 (2005).

The purpose of this article is to provide a snapshot of assessment practices for distance MBA programs in order to help readers gain a better understanding of this landscape. We envision that these findings will help institutions involved with distance MBA programs strengthen their assessment strategies.

With nearly thirty years of combined experience with master's degree programs in business administration, we have been concerned with assessment questions for quite some time. More recently, we have had increasing levels of involvement with MBA curricular issues and program assessment at Colorado State University, including developing program assessment for the College of Business's disciplinary accreditation efforts. The MBA program with which we are associated has a large distance component, which led to our curiosity about the state of assessment for distance MBA programs.

"The term distance education has been applied to a tremendous variety of programs serving numerous audiences via a wide variety of media" (Palloff and Pratt, 1999, p. 8). For the purposes of our study, an MBA distance education program is defined as any MBA program in which (1) all or most (more than 50 percent) of the instruction and interaction among faculty, students, and administrators takes place on a basis that is other than face to face; that is, students are not co-located with the instructor or necessarily with one another; (2) instruction is synchronous or asynchronous; (3) instruction occurs via the World Wide Web, DVD or videotape distribution, distribution of printed materials, or the use of specialized communication software (for example, Blackboard, Embanet, Web CT, or Net-Meeting); and (4) the program uses e-mail or faxes for communication between students and faculty, students and students, and students and administrators.

Method

We designed a nineteen-item on-line questionnaire that surveyed distance MBA providers in regard to their assessment practices. The survey solicited the following information:

- Who is assessed?
- What is the most common measure used?
- What additional measures are used?
- When are assessments conducted?
- What is done with the information obtained?
- Are MBA assessment strategies for distance programs the same as those conducted on campus? If so, how?
- How would respondents improve their assessment practices?

Sample

To identify our sample, we developed a list of 183 MBA coordinators and MBA advisers using the following resources: 2002 Peterson's Guide to MBA Programs; "GetEducated! Best Distance Learning Graduate Schools—Business & Management 2002" <www.geteducated.com>; the "Top Techno-MBA Programs 2002" list in *Computerworld* magazine; and the *U.S. News and World Report 2002 E-Learning Directory*. Our response rate was 33 percent (sixty institutions). Of those responding, twenty institutions indicated that they did not have a distance MBA program, according to our definition.

Results

Who is assessed? Students, faculty, employers, and alumni are targeted in the assessment practices of distance MBA programs.

What is the most common measure used? Measuring satisfaction is the most common assessment practice. Students are most often asked about their satisfaction with the overall program (95 percent), followed by their satisfaction with faculty (92.5 percent) and their satisfaction with technology (75 percent). Nearly half of respondents indicated that they assess faculty satisfaction with curriculum. Approximately one-third of our respondents ask employers about their satisfaction with the MBA program and with graduates.

What additional measures are used? Graduation rates, job placement rates, and student salaries after placement were the most frequently mentioned nonsatisfaction measures. Two-thirds of our respondents used written surveys (rather than on-line surveys) to assess their distance MBA program.

When are assessments conducted? Ninety percent of our respondents indicated that they conduct assessments at the end of a course or term; 63 percent occur at the end of the program, while still fewer are conducted after graduation (25 percent).

What is done with the information obtained? Our respondents indicated that assessment results are most frequently used to make curricular changes (85 percent). Revising admission standards, upgrading technology, changing faculty, and providing teaching awards were also identified as reasons for conducting assessments.

Are MBA assessment strategies for distance programs the same as those conducted on campus? If so, how? We found that nearly half of the respondents undertake program assessment differently for their distance programs than they do for their on-campus programs. In the distance programs, for example, assessment efforts focus on the overall graduate education experience, results are shared with more campus personnel, and the assessments include more questions about pedagogy and interactivity than do their on-campus counterparts.

How would respondents improve their assessment practices? Suggestions for improving assessment practices included increasing the level of sophistication of assessment strategies, developing a more comprehensive articulation of student learning outcomes along with accompanying assessment of those outcomes, and increasing follow-up with program alumni and with students who withdraw from the MBA program.

Several respondents advocated increased involvement of employers in the assessment effort. Such assessments might include employers' perceptions of the value and relevance of MBA enrollment as well as a longitudinal assessment of MBA graduates.

According to a survey conducted by the Graduate Management Admission Council and cited in *Selections* (Bruce, Edgington, and Olkin, 2003), the purpose of obtaining an MBA degree pertains mainly to professional development, including enhancing one's marketability, increasing earning power, and changing careers. However, our findings indicate that only 40 percent of our respondents measure student perceptions of professional development. Less than one-third of our respondents indicated that they measure student salaries after placement. Eighteen percent ask whether employers are satisfied with the graduates. Approximately 10 percent ask about student satisfaction with job placement after graduation.

Conclusion

Our research indicates that current assessment efforts for distance MBA programs leave significant room for improvement. Garrison and Anderson (2003) state, "Judging the worth of an e-learning experience is a broad and complex topic that includes much more than merely assessing student performance outcomes and their [students'] perceptions of the value of the course" (p. 104). Most of our respondents used student satisfaction measures as the principal assessment tool. Research on these types of self-report measures does not support their use as an exclusive or even a reliable assessment strategy (Palloff and Pratt, 1999, p. 157).

As universities seek to draw additional students via distance education, a more standardized definition of distance learning needs to be established. Significantly more sophisticated efforts to assess program goal accomplishments are essential. Exploring why assessment practices for distance programs are so different from those for on-campus programs is another area for further research.

"Legitimate institutions have expended considerable effort to demonstrate the quality of their distance education programs" (Palloff and Pratt, 1999, p. 16). Our conclusion is that they still have a long way to go.

Acknowledgment

Data on which this article is based were first presented at the 2002 Assessment Institute in Indianapolis, Indiana.

References

Bruce, G. D., Edgington, R., and Olkin, J. M. "Apply and Demand: How the Economy Affects Graduates' Career Choices." *Selections*, Spring 2003, pp. 5–11. [http://www.gmac.com/selections/spring2003/index.html].

Garrison, D. R., and Anderson, T. *E-Learning in the 21st Century: A Framework for Research and Practice*. New York: RoutledgeFalmer, 2003.

Palloff, R. M., and Pratt, K. *Building Learning Communities in Cyberspace*. San Francisco: Jossey-Bass, 1999.

In 2005, James A. McCambridge was associate professor of management and Kathy L. Thornhill was advising services coordinator in the College of Business at Colorado State University in Fort Collins, Colorado.

Assessment in Disciplines Not Subject to Accreditation

Assessment of the Major at Virginia Commonwealth University: Two Examples

Barbara S. Fuhrmann

Look for: Assessment methods in history and urban studies and planning. History majors develop a portfolio, while the knowledge, skills, and attitudes of urban studies and planning majors are assessed via open-ended questionnaires for entering students and graduating seniors. From Assessment Update 8:5 (1996).

Assessment of the major is an important challenge for all university faculty. Here I provide two examples of successful efforts in which faculty became committed to assessment. In each case, the assessment strategies selected had relevance to teaching and the assessment coordinator was a faculty member in the department. Institutional support in the form of release time for the coordinator was also important to the success of these two programs.

Example 1: Assessing the History Major

Background and Purpose. All major field programs at Virginia Commonwealth University (VCU) are required to develop comprehensive assessment programs addressing both field-specific and general education outcomes. The history faculty soon became aware that its first task was to agree on expected student outcomes in history, and then to design an assessment strategy or strategies to measure student attainment of the outcomes.

Method. A full year's work went into developing five comprehensive knowledge and skill outcomes common to all graduating history majors. These concern both field-specific and general education outcomes as they are applied in the major. The assessment plan centers around the evaluation of portfolios compiled on the work of students in advanced seminars. The approach involves data collection, data evaluation, analysis and discussion of results, and the use of results in program modifications. The members of the department assessment committee read and evaluate the collected materials using an evaluation scale developed to correspond to the five essential goals for the history major.

Findings. The department faculty have not only identified areas of program strength and weakness but are demonstrating the power of assessment when it is woven into the continuing processes of the department. The assessment project has become a central focus of pedagogical discussion and curriculum revision.

Use of Findings. Information gathered through the assessment program has led to increasing scrutiny of the curriculum through discussion of implications and possible directions for helping students achieve the department goals for their learning. With an increasing number of faculty in a large department being drawn into the assessment process, the discussion has widened to encompass the entire curriculum and a new understanding of the department's place in the total scheme of curriculum change within the college. The department has demonstrated an honest attempt to reallocate existing resources to help majors reach the educational goals set for them by the faculty.

Success Factors. The identification of one faculty member with an interest in assessment and the appointment of that person as chair of the department assessment committee were key factors in the success of the project. Provision by the campus assessment office of release time for this individual to lead the development of the project allowed him the time to think critically about the program, its faculty, and its students. The provision of technical assistance to the faculty in the development of student learning outcomes and portfolio development and assessment assisted in their creation of a meaningful strategy. The dean recognized the value of the project and presented it as exemplary to the rest of the college.

Example 2: Assessing the Urban Studies and Planning Major

Background and Purpose. As one of many aspects of the assessment initiative in the bachelor's program in urban studies and planning, the faculty decided to survey entering and exiting students in an attempt to assess student knowledge, values, and skills related to 16 of 32 expected student outcomes. This strategy, as well as three others, including comprehensive assessment of students' writing competence, were developed in response to the challenge to develop a comprehensive assessment strategy addressing both general education and major field outcomes.

Method. The faculty developed a ten-item open-ended survey requiring written responses and addressing the knowledge, skills, and attitudes related to the physical environment of the city; urbanization; urban economy; urban sociology; demographics; political processes; relationships among physical, economic, social, and political forces; and major problems of cities. The format of the survey allowed also for analysis of written communication skills, quantitative analysis skills, reasoning skills, organizational presentation skills, critical thinking, understanding of complexity, ethical dimensions of social conflict, and understanding of diverse cultural perspectives. Although administered on a pilot basis to graduating students, it was soon expanded and given to entering students as well. Each year a three-hour faculty meeting is devoted to analyzing assessment findings. Graduating students contribute by commenting on, affirming, or modifying faculty observations, as well as by offering their own evaluations of the program.

Findings. Surveys pointed out specific deficiencies in student knowledge, skills, and attitudes at graduation. These weaknesses were further analyzed by giving the surveys to entering students and documenting the level of knowledge and skills at time of program entry. Analysis of skill levels indicated a need for greater attention to written communication skills and to ethical dimensions of decision making and problem solving within the context of the major.

Use of Findings. Results have led to a number of changes. First, the attendance at the orientation program is now compulsory. Second, an evaluation form for written work is used by all program faculty to provide feedback on writing in program courses and thereby to focus on development of knowledge and skills in need of strengthening. Third, there is now a programwide faculty effort in developing ethical decision-making skills.

Success Factors. The program faculty appointed an assessment coordinator with interest in assessment, the assessment office provided several semesters of release time for him to develop and implement the program, and the program faculty devoted monthly faculty meetings to exploring all aspects of assessment and developed a comprehensive list of expected student outcomes. Commitment from the dean resulted in publicizing of the comprehensive assessment plan as exemplary throughout the professional school. The involvement of students in the development and evaluation of the strategy provided a valuable perspective and eventually resulted in high student commitment to improving both the assessment program and the academic experience of students.

Barbara S. Fuhrmann was director of academic planning at Virginia Commonwealth University, Richmond, at the time these programs were developed.

Capstones and Quality: The Culminating Experience as Assessment

Billy Catchings

Look for: Assessment in communication via a Web-based capstone course. Seniors compile portfolios, reflecting on the content as evidence of their development of specified learning outcomes, then work together to plan an event at which their projects are presented and evaluated by faculty. From Assessment Update *16:1 (2004).*

Assessment! Perhaps no word in academe has loomed more dauntingly than the much-feared "A" word. Several years ago, my institution embarked on its self-study for North Central Association accreditation with the issue of quality assessment linked to outcomes ringing loudly in our collective ears. As Massy (2003) explains, defining quality in terms of outcomes means describing student learning and its consequences. All academic units at the University of Indianapolis were faced with the reality of demonstrating outcomes-oriented evaluation of student learning. The Department of Communication was no exception. A few of the academic units at our medium-sized private university of just under four thousand students had already developed capstone experiences, prompted by the demands of professional certifications and licensures. Departments in the College of Arts and Sciences, however, had not yet begun to achieve widespread compliance with the capstone trend.

After an extensive audit of our curriculum in connection with the university self-study, the communication faculty agreed to implement a multifaceted senior project that would serve in two capacities: (1) as a culminating experience wherein students would engage in reflective analysis of their education and (2) as a quality assessment tool to satisfy the standards of accreditation. The decision to adopt a final project with a critical, reflective component coheres with the views of Harris and Sansom (2000), who offer four academic applications of Schön's principles of reflective practice to facilitate faculty use of tacit knowledge and to improve student learning and institutional practices. I will briefly describe our capstone experience as a reflective practice, explain its utility in assessment and improving quality, and identify some of the challenges we have encountered and continue to address.

The Capstone: A Senior Project

The Department of Communication organizes its course of study into six major areas: electronic media, journalism, human communication, public relations, corporate communication, and sports information. Students select courses in their major areas but are required to complete a departmental core that introduces them to all of the subdisciplines as well as to the essential elements of research, writing, law, and practical application. We wanted the senior project to be indicative of and consistent with both the specialized and integrative nature of the undergraduate program. The planning produced a one-credit-hour capstone experience that includes the following elements:

- A Web-based course in which students and instructor interact weekly and meet as needed for eleven to twelve weeks
- Development of individual portfolios that are submitted to a faculty jury
- Planning and deployment of a senior event featuring individual presentations adjudicated by faculty

The Web-Based Course. Despite some initial reservations on the part of faculty and staff, the on-line dimension of the course proved satisfactory to both students and instructors. The course is administered on Blackboard, a class bulletin board and chat room where students access the syllabus and, along with the instructor, engage in weekly discussions. Points are awarded based on regular participation in the on-line discussion. The primary purpose of the interactions is to provide a forum in which students seek and exchange advice on the preparation of their portfolio and their presentation. The on-line discussions are also used to plan the senior project event.

The Portfolio. Determining what the portfolio should contain and how it would be evaluated presented a challenge. At first, faculty were quite ambitious in regard to the contents. Ultimately, we agreed on core submissions (cover letter, résumé, and samples of expository or critical writing) and representative works reflecting accomplishments (manuscripts, production tapes, news clippings, designs, and so on) in the students' major subdisciplines. Each submission must be prefaced with a written reflection that includes the submission's origin as well as a self-assessment of the learning it demonstrates. The reflective piece is intended to distinguish the portfolio from a repository or scrapbook, which would serve as a mere collection of materials rather than an assessment document. Portfolios are distributed to a three-member faculty jury, which employs collaboratively developed criteria and rubrics for grading.

The Senior Project Event. During the online discussions, students swap ideas and make final plans for the senior project event. This aspect of the capstone is intended to foster collaborative planning and teamwork as students design the agenda, then plan, promote, and implement the program. The centerpiece for the event is a series of presentations given by students. Students prepare and deliver speeches that are designed to demonstrate competence in topic development, technological support, and oral communication. The faculty as jury evaluate and assign grades to the presentations as well as the overall event.

The Senior Project as Assessment

The utility of the capstone experience in assessing the quality of the Department of Communication's academic program has been excellent. After completion of the senior project sequence and upon final grading of the portfolios, the presentations, and the event, department faculty convene to debrief and reflect on the quality of the senior project. Ultimately, the discussions reveal connections (or disconnections) between the capstone and the department course of study. Tagg (2003) notes, "Characterizing the challenge of alignment isn't the same thing as meeting the challenge, but it is probably a useful first step" (p. 284).

Each spring at the department review and planning retreat, faculty devote substantial time to developing strategies for improvement based on evaluations of the senior project. The issues of alignment among curriculum, learning, and the capstone have prompted concerted efforts to improve the quality of both the curriculum and the capstone. Among the changes that have been implemented are the following:

- Redesign of department core curriculum courses in order to reinforce expectations in writing and oral communication

- Standardization of syllabi to identify work in courses that satisfies portfolio requirements
- Introduction of faculty consultations with seniors regarding topics for student presentations

The preceding examples illustrate a few of our efforts to address what Tagg (2003) describes as the misalignment of existing structures. Addressing points of misalignment has been our greatest challenge in maintaining and improving the capstone experience. Initially, I believe, we envisioned and designed the capstone as a disembodied performance without deeply exploring the extent of its alignment with student learning. Disappointments and dissatisfactions with portfolios and presentations heralded the reality that there exist points of incongruence that must be addressed continually. We were and still are faced with the need to honestly identify how well our students have learned what we think we have taught them. We have had to consider how capable they are in demonstrating or performing that learning in a culminating and synthesizing experience. The Senior Project has enlightened and discouraged us but has ultimately reinforced our resolve to address misalignment. To borrow from Tagg (2003) again, our commitment to aligning the capstone with student learning is one realization of our pledge to strive for quality improvement and systematic integrity.

References

Harris, J., and Sansom, D. *Discerning Is More Than Counting.* AALE Occasional Papers in Liberal Education, no. 3. Washington, D.C.: American Academy for Liberal Education, 2000.

Massy, W. F. *Honoring the Trust: Quality and Cost Containment in Higher Education.* Bolton, MA: Anker, 2003.

Tagg, J. The Learning Paradigm College. Bolton, MA: Anker, 2003.

In 2004, Billy Catchings was associate professor and chair of the Department of Communication at the University of Indianapolis.

Assessment Outcomes Confirm the Value of a University's Required Fitness/Wellness Course

Gwen C. Robbins, Debbie Powers, Jerry Rushton

Look for: Evaluation of the effectiveness of a fitness/wellness course using a test of knowledge, an opinionnaire probing students' appraisals of the course, a life-style questionnaire, and a series of tests of cardiorespiratory endurance. From Assessment Update 4:5 (1992).

According to the Ball State University undergraduate catalogue, a central purpose of general education is "to enable men and women to live rich and satisfying lives." Since 1985 physical education has been included as part of the required general studies core for all undergraduate students at Ball State. Serving a student population of approximately 19,000, the physical education component of the current requirement is two semester hours. This requirement consists of a two-hour Physical Education Fitness/ Wellness course (hereafter referred to as PEFWL) that combines physical fitness activity and integrated lecture topics related to wellness.

The PEFWL course uses a two-fold approach: (1) a series of classroom lectures that cover a variety of wellness topics; and (2) laboratory activity sessions, where progress is made toward achieving physical fitness through a specific aerobic activity. Each student enrolls in PEFWL according to the desired aerobic activity. The selections include physical conditioning, fitness walking, jogging, swimnastics, rhythmic aerobics, bicycling, and fitness swimming. One 50-minute class per week is spent in a large lecture (90–125 students). Two times per week the student attends his or her activity lab with the 20 to 30 other students who have selected that aerobic activity.

With this design, the student completes the 16-week semester, obtaining proficiency, guidance, and self-confidence in a specific aerobic activity.

The activity lab also allows the student to assess personal fitness levels and needs, develop other health-related fitness components, and gain an appreciation of the impact physical fitness has in the pursuit of wellness.

Faculty teaching the seven PEFWL courses perceived that the courses were making a positive impact on the lives of students, but this perception had never been tested. As the program evolved, other pertinent questions arose: Are these courses having any effects on students' lives? Are the students acquiring knowledge of fitness/wellness? Do cardiorespiratory endurance levels and flexibility improve? How are resting heart rates and blood pressures affected? Does body weight or body composition change? In short, are we doing what we say we are doing? During the spring semester of 1989, a project team was assembled to assess the PEFWL courses and address these questions.

The Assessment Project

Approximately 1,500 students were randomly selected from sections of the PEFWL course offerings and were assessed before and after the course to determine knowledge gained during the course, attitude toward the course, current lifestyle, and changes in physical fitness that occurred while they were enrolled.

The knowledge test consisted of 50 multiple-choice questions based on material from the textbook and lecture series. An opinionnaire, designed to examine the student's attitude toward both the activity lab and the lecture, was administered to all students during the physical fitness post-testing session. A 25-item life-style questionnaire was designed to measure current health habits of students. A follow-up administration of the life-style questionnaire to a randomly selected sample of alumni who took this course will be conducted to see whether permanent life-style changes have occurred.

Because of the large number of physical fitness variables to be tested, the project team trained a group of faculty, graduate students, and undergraduate students to assist with the assessment. The battery of tests was designed to measure the following elements: body weight, blood pressure, body composition (Sloan formula), muscular strength and endurance (one-minute timed abdominal curls, one-minute timed pushups), flexibility (sit and reach), and cardiorespiratory endurance.

The tests for cardiorespiratory endurance were activity-specific. Aerobic dance and jogging students performed the one-and-a-half-mile run, while fitness-walking students were tested on the one-mile walk. Bicycling students were timed on a five-mile ride, and fitness swimmers performed a five-hundred-yard swim. Swimnastics students completed the new five-hundred-yard water walk/run. Both pre- and post-tests were conducted by trained personnel using the same protocol, equipment, and testing facilities.

Assessment Results

Seventy percent (1,144) of the students in the computer-selected courses completed both pre- and post-testing. Pre-and post-test findings revealed significant improvement in almost all the physical variables that were examined. The 50-item multiple-choice test also showed significant improvement in students' knowledge. The type of course did not influence the outcome measures; that is, students in PEFWL Jogging performed no differently from students in PEFWL Fitness Walking or any other course.

Implications

This assessment project confirmed that each PEFWL course is improving cardiorespiratory endurance—a primary goal of the program—and that students are acquiring basic fitness/wellness knowledge. The study suggested a need to investigate special populations within the PEFWL courses. For instance, what is happening to students over the age of 24? Are students with obesity problems making any physical change? There will be a need to follow up with a long-range life-style assessment. How will these same students respond years later? Moreover, the assessment project should be replicated using the same format to determine the reliability of these findings.

Although the assessment project was a massive undertaking, the outcomes have been valuable to both students and faculty. Faculty have been assured that their efforts are having a positive impact on the present and, they hope, the future lives of their students. Furthermore, on several commonly used fitness tests the project has led to improvements that have been of great value to physical education teachers and students.

Those conducting the assessment project are convinced that a physical education course of this design, in which students focus on one aerobic activity per semester, is superior to courses that offer a smorgasbord approach, such as two weeks of one activity followed by two weeks of another. Students enrolled for the semester in one fitness activity may develop expertise not gained in a sampling of various activities. In this fitness/wellness course students develop an understanding of the "gain without pain" concept and discover that exercise can be enjoyable and social. Ball State students are learning that aerobic exercise is a lifetime activity and that when combined with other wellness habits, it is helping students explore their potential.

In 1992, Gwen C. Robbins was director of the Fitness, Sports, and Leisure Studies Program, Ball State University; Debbie Powers was assistant professor, School of Physical Education, Ball State University; and Jerry Rushton was associate professor, School of Physical Education, Ball State University.

Assessment through the Senior Letter

Virginia McKinley, Spencer A. McWilliams

Look for: Assessment across majors using a senior letter. Upon applying to graduate, seniors are asked to write a letter responding to specific questions about their college experiences. Content analysis of these responses suggests needed improvements, examples of which are cited. From Assessment Update *4:6 (1992).*

For over twenty years, since Warren Wilson College began awarding the baccalaureate degree, students have applied for degree candidacy by writing a letter to the faculty and staff of the college. The dean of the college requests the letter and specifies the types of information to be included. The letter is submitted to the faculty of the student's major department, who verify that the candidate has completed all requirements for graduation and determine whether to recommend the candidate for the degree.

The senior letter was not originally designed specifically as an assessment instrument, but the information requested from students has lent itself well to outcome assessment, particularly in terms of the general educational goals of the institution. One benefit of the senior letter format is that it provides a regular opportunity to gather student responses that might otherwise be reported only informally and anecdotally.

Beginning with the 1990–91 academic year, instructions for the Warren Wilson College senior letters were revised and expanded to solicit more systematic assessment information. The coordinator of academic planning and improvement conducted a detailed content analysis of all letters from the December 1990 and May 1991 graduates (a total of eighty-nine students). A report based on this analysis has been used by the president and the dean of the college as well as an academic program planning task force. It will also be used by members of all principal committees for the upcoming institutional self-study for accreditation, and it is anticipated that a similar content analysis will be prepared in future years as a continuing aid to institutional planning and assessment.

In addition to pursuing their academic studies, all resident students at Warren Wilson College are required to work fifteen hours per week in the college work program, and all students are required to complete a minimum of twenty hours per year of community service. Therefore, in their senior letters students are asked to discuss their course experiences and their service projects, providing a global survey of educational activities for their careers at the college. Seniors are also asked to discuss their plans following graduation and to evaluate the general outcomes of their education. Finally, they are asked to assess their overall experience at the college. Specifically, they are asked to comment on what has been of special value to them, what contributions they have made to the college and to their education, how they may have been disappointed, and what recommendations they might make for the future of the college.

After the faculty of the major departments have read the letters, they are placed on file at the registrar's office, where they are available for review by all members of the college faculty, staff, and administration.

Analysis of recurrent themes in student suggestions or criticisms has helped to develop a more objective sense of how students perceive the college. Senior letters have also yielded information that has been of use to the faculty in revising curriculum and major programs. For instance, students have particularly appreciated opportunities for experimental or "hands-on" learning. Forestry students praise a summer course that includes daily field experience, integrates work and study, and leads to practical results: a management plan for part of the college's seven hundred acres of forest. Education majors mention the value of student teaching and the practicum course at the campus Early Learning Center. Students in the humanities mention independent research projects, as do students in the sciences. Undergraduate science projects are often funded by outside grants, and students generally approve of the requirement (and the challenge) to make a public presentation of their research results as part of the Natural Science Seminar.

Seniors consistently report that work and service are among their most important learning opportunities. They also clearly learn through living in a small campus community much of what other colleges and universities attempt to address through their general education programs. Thus senior letters suggest that a number of transferable skills and competencies are potentially developed outside the classroom, and the letters underscore the need to continue articulating those skills and competencies, coordinating opportunities for developing them, and encouraging faculty, staff, and students to reflect more consciously on the process of developing them.

Senior letters confirmed a general sense among faculty and staff that the service learning program was weaker and less important to the students than the academic and work programs. As a result, in the spring of 1990 the service program was strengthened. The director's position was increased from half-time to full-time; students are now required to complete a minimum of twenty hours of service each year, rather than the previous requirement of only one sixty-hour project; and the new service director has developed more opportunities for students to reflect directly on their service experience.

Over the years, information gleaned from senior letters has influenced the development of the college's curriculum and academic programs in several ways. For example, a required capstone course for all seniors was instituted several years ago following enthusiastic response to a course in autobiographies. A significant number of seniors suggested that this course should be required of all students. These comments stimulated faculty discussion leading to development of the two principal elements of the Senior Seminar: an autobiography and a personal credo.

Curriculum planning within the majors has frequently benefited from information in the senior letters. For instance, in response to consistently expressed enthusiasm for field learning, the environmental studies program has maintained and expanded field learning courses, both on and off the campus. Most frequently mentioned as "the best experience" or "my most memorable academic experience" is Discovery Through Wilderness, an interdisciplinary course in wilderness ecology that includes a month-long trip to a wilderness area. Although the course requires considerable faculty time, it has recently been expanded from an alternate-year to an annual offering.

Senior letters also demonstrated that, although environmental studies students had a good background in the natural sciences, many had a poor grasp of the economic, political, and cultural complexities involved in reducing pollution or preserving natural areas. As a result, two capstone courses—Environmental Policy, and Community and Regional Studies—which focus on the economic, political, and cultural dimensions of environmental management, were added to the curriculum.

According to senior letters written several years ago, the intercultural studies major lacked coherent focus. The program had been designed with required foundation courses plus a concentration, but the possible concentrations had not been clearly defined by the program, and students often completed the major with a nearly random selection of forty credit hours.

Subsequently, five clearly defined concentrations were developed, and students now also receive more guidance in planning their major programs and in writing a formal proposal clarifying the focus of their studies.

Several senior letters from students majoring in intercultural studies further indicated the special significance of the opportunity to work and study abroad through the college's international development program. As a result, an extended cross-cultural experience—which could be an international development group project, individual work and study abroad, or a domestic cross-cultural experience (for instance, the Appalachian Term field study course or work in refugee communities)—became a requirement for the intercultural studies major. Students also indicated that their experience abroad would have been even more beneficial had they had better language preparation. For that reason, a foreign-language prerequisite and course requirement were added to the major.

The more systematic analysis of 1990–91 senior letters substantiated many of the general impressions from prior years and confirmed the importance of several current planning and curriculum review processes. It indicated general satisfaction with the selection and quality of elective and core courses. When seniors recall their most valuable learning experiences at the college, they mention courses and personalities that are representative of all areas of the educational program. In fact, many seniors identify as most valuable a variety of courses not directly related to their majors or minors. Students particularly appreciate their elective options because some of their most satisfying courses have been in areas of the curriculum whose appeal they had not anticipated before enrolling in those classes. However, the 1990–91 graduates did not seem to distinguish between core and elective courses and showed no particular awareness of the "ways of knowing" theme for the Warren Wilson core. Thus senior letters confirmed the importance of a reassessment of the structure and objectives of the general education program. Such a review is in progress.

One general education requirement is a one-term composition course, but faculty members reading senior letters consistently note that the quality of student writing does not always meet their expectations for college seniors. In addition, some seniors have specifically requested an increased emphasis on language and communication skills and a greater variety of writing courses that are not necessarily oriented toward the study of literature. Therefore, a yearlong, first-year writing and oral communication sequence is now under serious consideration by the academic planning bodies, as is a proposal for a new faculty position in rhetoric and composition.

These various analyses, across several years, have demonstrated the utility of the senior letter as an assessment tool. The letters often confirm the general perceptions held by administrators, faculty, and students regarding the strengths and weaknesses of academic programs and their staffing and curriculum design. Yet the letters also provide some unanticipated information that has been used regularly over the years for planning and improvement and will be used more systematically for these purposes in the future. Senior letters undoubtedly will continue to prove useful for eliciting general information about students' perceptions of the educational program, information that can complement the more analytical and data-oriented measures ordinarily used in outcome assessment.

In 1992, Virginia McKinley was coordinator for academic assessment and Spencer A. McWilliams was vice president for academic affairs and dean of the college, Warren Wilson College.

Assessing Student Learning in Graduate Programs

Patricia D. Murphy

Look for: Assessment in graduate education. Faculty have identified four common outcomes for all graduate programs, and they apply rubrics to traditional student work products such as term papers, course exams, theses, and oral presentations to assess student attainment of these outcomes. From Assessment Update 6:6 (1994).

The assessment of student academic achievement is being expanded at North Dakota State University (NDSU) to include the learning of students in graduate programs. Content analysis of departmental assessment plans for the 40 master's degree programs (M.A., M.S., M.Ed., and M.B.A.) and the 19 doctoral programs (Ph.D.) identified four common intended student outcomes: (1) communicate effectively in written and oral forms, (2) solve problems related to the field, (3) carry out research projects, and (4) demonstrate knowledge in the field. The ways in which departments proposed to assess these outcomes were also fairly common across programs: (1) preparation of case studies, term papers, or projects in courses; (2) exam questions in courses; (3) oral seminar presentations; (4) comprehensive written exams; (5) research proposals; (6) dissertations, theses, scientific papers, or comprehensive study papers; and (7) final oral exams (defense of paper, thesis, or dissertation).

Faculty involved with graduate programs know how to make judgments about the work of individual students. They regularly make such decisions in giving grades in graduate courses, administering comprehensive exams, approving the research proposal, and declaring the thesis or dissertation acceptable. In these decisions, faculty are making judgments about students as individuals.

Faculty at NDSU did not wish to abandon the traditional hallmarks of graduate education, such as the written comprehensive exams, research proposals, and theses. They also did not wish to create a new system to assess program outcomes. The task became one of determining how to use what was already in place for the additional purpose of assessing program outcomes in order to improve student learning.

For example, the fact that ten students successfully completed all requirements for the master's degree in computer science told the department faculty nothing about strengths or weaknesses of their degree program. It provided no clues as to which part or parts of the program (if any) needed improvement. Likewise, grades of A or B in courses provided faculty with no evidence of areas of need or strength. As a result, faculty decided it was necessary to look at these in-place activities in new ways. One answer seemed to be checklists to use with the already curriculum-embedded activities.

In all our graduate programs, essay exam questions, term papers, master's theses, and dissertations are used as evidence of achievement of graduate-level communication outcomes. The question became, "How do you go beyond the decision of a pass/fail, a grade, or a score on these activities?" The faculty determined that graduate students must be able to identify and analyze problems, to criticize and apply existing knowledge, to attempt new solutions, and to produce convincing presentations of results.

However, what currently happens in most graduate programs is that faculty simply approve or disapprove the final oral examination. They do the same for the thesis and dissertation. Since the primary goal of assessment is to improve student learning, the critical issue is taking the next step, getting beyond evaluating the work of individual students merely to assign grades or to say "they pass" so they can have the degree they desire, to collecting data for use in identifying areas of strength in the program and areas needing improvement.

One suggestion is to break the activity into component parts. What are the skills and abilities the faculty expect the graduate student to demonstrate in the oral presentation? In the written thesis or dissertation? In the final defense? The faculty then create a list of parts of the activity related to the intended student outcomes. Attached to each activity is a simple rating scale, such as outstanding, satisfactory, or inadequate. Student names are not needed. The faculty complete the rating at the same time as the activity, the oral seminar presentation, the faculty reading of the research proposal, or the final defense of the paper. The lists are examined once or twice a year, depending on the number of students. A departmental review committee can look at the rating sheets to begin to identify patterns of strength and areas where improvement may be needed. This has nothing to do with a student's grade in a course or ability to graduate, and faculty do not have to read entire papers or exams again. It is possible for graduate faculty to engage in meaningful assessment without excessive burden and within current graduate education practices.

In 1994, Patricia D. Murphy was dean of assessment and institutional research at North Dakota State University, Fargo.

Standardized Measures of Student Learning in the Major

Public Reporting of Teacher Pass Rates: Anomaly or Precedent?

Peter T. Ewell

Look for: Analysis of the use of standard measures within states to assess the competence of majors in teacher education. Is public disclosure of institutions' passing rates in teacher education an anomaly, or will requirements for using standardized tests and reporting institutions' aggregate scores be imposed in other fields? From Assessment Update 14:4 (2002).

Teacher education has long been higher education's leading edge with respect to state-level accountability based on standardized testing. While only six or seven states have used testing as a general-purpose accountability mechanism for public colleges and universities in the last two decades, more than half of the states have employed this device to hold teacher training programs accountable. In part, this is because data on graduate performance are readily available. As in many other professions, including medicine and law, teachers must be licensed to practice by passing state-established examinations. But the examination systems for teachers are run directly by an arm of government—usually the state's department of education. This makes it far easier to use the resulting data not only to certify individuals to practice, but also to hold publicly funded teacher education programs accountable by applying the data in the aggregate. At least as important, teacher education is the part of higher education that is most visibly connected to the K–12 arena, where the use of test-based accountability as a policy tool is both familiar and formidable. Virtually every state has now adopted some form of senior-level assessment as a condition of exit from high school, and the education bill passed by Congress this year and championed by the Bush White House has made this practice far more salient for policymakers. Its logic is simple: schools whose graduates perform poorly on such examinations should be cited, and perhaps sanctioned, by those responsible for governing and funding them; parents and communities, in turn, should be apprised of poor performance and provided an opportunity to send their children elsewhere.

For over a year, teacher education programs at all U.S. colleges and universities receiving federal funds have been subject to the same kind of mandate through a federal provision known as Title II. Unfolding experience with this program is instructive, because it appears to have satisfied nobody. On the one hand, K–16 reformers who believe that publicly reported data about comparative performance constitute a useful lever for program improvement are disappointed that states can't really be compared, and they want to fix this "problem." On the other hand, those in the academy who resist any form of test-based accountability on the grounds that it yields little information about actual program performance see such provisions as the "camel's nose" of a broader and more dangerous federal accountability agenda for higher education. From either viewpoint, examining Title II is instructive, as it could be a sign of things to come.

Congress enacted Title II, Section 207, as part of the 1998 Amendments to the Higher Education Act (HEA) in order to designate new appropriations to improve teacher education programs. Requiring colleges and universities to report annual pass rates on state licensure examinations for prospective teachers was part of this overall improvement package, intended to provide appropriate accountability for new money. In addition, reporting widely and consistently was supposed to stimulate better performance. The logic behind this measure was thus consistent not only with contemporary approaches to K–12 policy, but also with long-established federal performance-reporting requirements such as Student Right-to-Know, which has required public reporting of crime statistics and graduation rates since 1989.

Though taken somewhat by surprise by Title II (much as they were by the State Postsecondary Review Entities amendments in 1992), the higher education lobbying community resisted its provisions on the usual grounds: excessive complexity, reporting burden on institutions, and the unreliability of any resulting data. The U.S. Department of Education (DOE), in turn, was slow to develop the regulations needed to implement the law, and this delayed the implementation of Title II by a year. To date, though, reporting has proceeded as scheduled. Institutions provided the required data to their state authorities in Spring 2001; summary statistics for each institution were published by each state in November; and the DOE produced an overall report on the program in April 2002.

Title II requires each institution that offers teacher education to report annually and publicly on the percentage of its graduates in teacher education who pass the examinations required by the state for licensure. It also requires each state to prepare a report on the comparative pass-rate performances of all institutions (both public and private). Pass rates are reported under six headings that aggregate similar tests: basic skills, professional knowledge, academic content, other content, special populations (such as ESL or special education), and performance assessments. General groupings like this were needed to make sense of the vastly different testing content requirements established by the various states. States are to report four things annually to the DOE and the public: (1) pass rates for each institution in each of the six performance categories and overall, (2) aggregated pass rates for the state as a whole, (3) a ranking of institutions into four performance quartiles, based on the overall pass rate, and (4) a designation of specific low-performing institutions (along with plans for improvement). Institutions, or state authorities operating on their behalf, are expected to obtain the required data directly from the testing companies involved, and according to the law, institutions can be fined up to $25,000 for noncompliance (a penalty waived by the DOE in the first year of implementation). But the measure does not include any way to sanction states that do not comply, nor can it sanction testing companies for not providing the required information.

As the first year of implementation demonstrates, Title II does not provide a way for the federal government to meaningfully compare the performances of individual colleges and universities in different states. But it does provide a highly visible mechanism for individual states to do so, if they choose. This is primarily because the requirements for teacher certification and licensure differ markedly between states. About ten states do not require any form of testing during teacher education; as a consequence, they have nothing to report. Other states require a test only to *enter* a teacher preparation program. Others will recommend a student for completion only after he or she has passed all the needed tests. Such states can choose to avoid meaningful reporting under Title II by establishing policies that teacher candidates must pass all of the tests needed for licensure before being recommended for completion. This defeats the intent of the law because all completing students will pass by definition. Because they set their own licensure requirements, states have the statutory right to do this, of course. And the best available evidence does suggest a trend in this direction since the establishment of Title II.

Even when states do require an exit test, the actual examinations they employ vary considerably, as do the performance levels they require to pass. Most states use tests supplied by the Educational Testing Service (primarily in the Praxis series), while a substantial minority of large states use tests supplied by National Evaluation Systems (NES). Cut scores also differ across states. Even states using examinations supplied by the same vendor may use different combinations or versions. NES, for example, makes the claim that its examinations are tailored to the standards set by each state (although considerations of both content and good business sense may cause a substantial empirical overlap among the examinations the company has developed). Even if all states established requirements for exit tests, therefore, results could not be compared meaningfully.

Despite its apparent failure as a blunt instrument of policy, Title II has had some important effects. First, systematic public disclosure of pass rates unquestionably has highlighted the poor performance of teacher education graduates. Press attention and the public nature of these reports means that digging deeper into this matter will be difficult for higher education to duck in the long run, even though the reports produced so far are not terribly meaningful. Sunshine laws and pressure from the media could, if exploited, force the disclosure of more detailed and revealing statistics.

Title II reporting has also uncovered the fact that there is no coherent or organized system for certifying teachers in the United States. Admittedly, statutory authority for certification—as well as the governance arrangements for delivering teacher education—likely will always reside at the state level. But the fact that the patchwork nature of current practice is now obvious to important observers could provide an occasion to surface this issue on a national basis. It could also provide an opportunity for a consortium of states to act together to align their standards, employ common tests, and report performance more consistently.

More important, Title II provides individual states with an opportunity to leverage a particular set of college and university programs aggressively in just the way they are now leveraging elementary and secondary schools. By forcing the disclosure of important statistics about graduate performance that up to now have not been available, and by taking advantage of the considerable latitude afforded by the law to identify and deal with low-performing institutions, states can potentially steer funds and students toward particular programs. Some states have taken advantage of this opportunity. Georgia, for instance, issued its own report card on teacher education in anticipation of Title II, using data already available. States like Texas and New York, in turn, have effectively used Title II reporting as a framework for organizing their own data-driven conversations about within-state performance and improvement.

What has higher education officials worried is that this same logic of public reporting and federal-state partnership could be applied to other fields. Events like last year's publication of *Measuring Up 2000*—the fifty-state report card on higher education that gave all states an "Incomplete" in student learning—have highlighted the topic of test-based performance measures in higher education for both the press and policy leaders. Meanwhile, the specter of a federal-state partnership to force the disclosure of many kinds of statistics about performance reminds some observers of SPRE—the State Postsecondary Review Entities established by the 1992 HEA amendments that caused higher education so much angst a decade ago. The reauthorization cycle for the HEA will begin again soon. In this context, the Bush administration has a clear preference for test-based accountability and may want to extend the logic of this mechanism up the educational ladder. However, the recently enacted education bill is already expensive, and that same administration, which has so far been remarkably focused with respect to its policy objectives, may allow higher education to sit this one out. Whichever way it comes out, examining Title II as an instance of a wider federal-state policy initiative is instructive because it remains a powerful example of both the power and complexity of test-based accountability at any level.

In 2002, Peter T. Ewell was vice president of the National Center for Higher Education Management Systems.